Dictionary of
Musical Terms

Da Capo Press Music Reprint Series

MUSIC EDITOR
BEA FRIEDLAND
Ph.D., City University of New York

Dictionary of Musical Terms

by Johannes Tinctoris

An English Translation of
TERMINORUM MUSICAE DIFFINITORIUM
Together with the Latin Text

Translated and Annotated
by
CARL PARRISH

DA CAPO PRESS·NEW YORK·1978

Library of Congress Cataloging in Publication Data

Tinctoris, Jean, d. 1511.
  Dictionary of musical terms = an English translation
of Terminorum musicae diffinitorium.

  (Da Capo Press music reprint series)
  Reprint of the 1963 ed. published by Free Press of
Glencoe, New York.
  1. Music—Terminology. 2. Music—Theory—
Medieval, 400-1500. I. Parrish, Carl.
  [ML108.T513 1978]   780'.3   77-26753
  ISBN 0-306-77560-3

DICTIONARY OF
MUSICAL TERMS

Submultiplex proportionû genus est : quo minor nûerus
ad maiorem relatus i illo mutilpliciter pcise continetur
ut unum ad duo & .i.ad.iii.

Superacuta loca & superacure uoces sunt ille & il'a:que
ab alamire su piori usqp ad e'a iclusiue i mâu côtinêur.

Supbiparties est proportio : qua maior nûerus ad miorem
relatus : illum in se totum côtinet & insuper duas eius
partes aliquotas unâ faciêtes aliquâram . ut .v.ad.iii.

Superparticulare ,pportionû genus est: quo maior nûe
rus ad minorem re'atus : illû in se totum continet : &
eius aliquâ partem aliquotâ. ut.iii.ad.ii.&.iiii.ad.iii.

Superparties ,pportionû genus e : quo maior numerus ad
minorem relatus : illû in se totum continet.& eius insu
per aliquas partes aliquotas : unâ facientes aliquâram .
ut quiqne ad tria. & .vii.ad.v.

Supposi: io est aliquorc corporum ut uoces loco notarum
significent introductio.

Supremum est illa pars cantus composui : quæ altitudine
cæteras excedit .

PER T CAPITVLVM .XVIII ::

T est litera quæ per se ad aliquam partem cantus posita :
tenorem istitutiôe significat. quæ quidê si prima sit mei
cognominis : quod Tinctoris est : mihi nô dedecori ue
nit quum & nomen domini ineffabile Tetagramaton
ab ea sumat exordium.

Talea est idemtitas particulare in una & eadem parte câ
tus existentium quoad nomen locum & ualorem nota
rum & pausare suare.

Dictionary of Musical Terms

by Johannes Tinctoris

An English Translation of

TERMINORUM MUSICAE DIFFINITORIUM

Together with the Latin Text

Translated and Annotated
by
CARL PARRISH

The Free Press of Glencoe
Collier-Macmillan Limited, London

10-09-78

To George Sherman Dickinson
with admiration and affection

PREFACE

Johannes Tinctoris (c. 1435-1511), the renowned musician and theorist of the early Renaissance, set forth his vast learning in an orderly series of twelve treatises, of which the *Terminorum musicae diffinitorium* ("Dictionary of Musical Terms," i.e., "of the terms used in music") is probably the first.* This work is the most famous of his books, and is the only one printed in his lifetime, except for some extracts from his last treatise, *De inventione et usu musicae,* c. 1484. The time of writing of the Dictionary is not known, but there are reasons for believing that it was compiled some time between 1474 and 1476.** It was probably shortly before it was written that Tinctoris entered the service of the King of Naples, Ferdinand I, in which it seems he remained for a period of nearly two decades; the treatises that followed the Dictionary were written during the first decade of that tenure. The prestige of the Dictionary, the time at which it was printed, and the many other bibliographical and typographical problems which the original printed edition has raised, have been fully and ably dealt with by my colleague, Mr. James B. Coover, in his essay that appears as an appendix to the present edition of the Dictionary. Mr. Coover is also responsible for the bibliography of the various manuscripts, copies of the original printed edition, and subsequent editions of the Dictionary which precede his essay.

The nearly 300 entries in the original edition of the Dictionary

---

* There is only one "Dictionary" of music known previously to Tinctoris' *Diffinitorium*—a *Vocabularium musicum* which is part of an eleventh-century manuscript. This contains 62 entries, many of which are names of instruments. It is reprinted in the *Essais de diphthérographie musicale* of Adrien de la Fage (Paris, 1862), pp. 404-407.

** Gustave Reese, *Music in the Renaissance.* New York, 1954, p. 140.

touch on a wide variety of matters concerning the musical theory and practice of Tinctoris' time, including the hexachord system, notation, proportions, intervals, acoustics, the church modes, musical forms, and a number of miscellaneous references to performance and related subjects. Some of the subjects entered are clearly defined, but many are cryptically brief and incomplete; some are found verbatim, or nearly so, in Tinctoris' subsequent treatises, while others are treated in the later volumes in minute detail.

Aside from the present work, modern translations of the Dictionary have been made in three different languages—German, French, and English. The first of these, by Heinrich Bellermann, appeared in the first issue of Chrysander's *Jahrbücher für musikalische Wissenschaft,* in 1863 (pp. 55-114). Bellermann's edition is based on the copy of the original printed edition at Gotha, and has a considerable number of valuable annotations, although his edition was made before the appearance of Coussemaker's *Scriptorum de musica medii aevi nova series* (1864-76), which contains, in Volume IV, all the treatises of Tinctoris except the last, and which would have made clear certain items about which Bellermann was in doubt. A French translation by Armand Machabey was published in 1951, with an instructive Introduction (xi-xxxix), and a small number of explanatory footnotes. Machabey's translation, though often quite free, is satisfactory on the whole. His reading of the Latin text is identical with that in Coussemaker (IV, pp. 177-191), which was made from a fifteenth-century manuscript in the Brussels *Bibliothèque Albert Ier* (the former *Bibliothèque Royale*) containing a few entries not in the original printed edition. An unpublished English translation made by Louis Balogh in 1940*** appears to be for the most part a translation of Bellermann.

The Latin text of the present edition follows closely that of the incunabulum in the British Museum, the only deviation from this being the correction of a few obvious minor misprints, a simplification of the punctuation, and the spelling out of the many abbreviations in the original printing. Certain orthographical usages of the period have been retained, such as "letitia" (laetitia) and

*** Master's Thesis, Western Reserve University.

"tercia" (tertia). Major errors occurring in the original have been left as they are, and are discussed in the notes. At the end of the Dictionary, a list of entries has been added which includes those in the Brussels manuscript but not in the printed edition, and also two further entries found only in a fifteenth-century manuscript of the Dictionary in the Library of the *Conservatorio di Musica G. B. Martini* at Bologna.

The present translation has been kept as literal as possible, although in some cases certain words have been added that seemed necessary to complete the meaning; where such additions verge upon interpretation they are enclosed in brackets. One of the difficulties in translation of works on music of this period is the ambiguous use of certain words. Notorious in this respect is *cantus,* which could serve many purposes, depending upon the context. In the Dictionary, the word appears to this writer to have been variously used for "music," "composition," "melody," "chant," and "song." Another such word is *vox,* which can mean both "voice" and "syllable" (i.e., "syllable of the hexachord"). The word *tonus* is another but, unlike *cantus* and *vox,* its different meanings (four in all) have been explained by Tinctoris himself. The use of the expression "Through A," etc., at the head of each "Chapter" may appear odd at first; it seemed better to use a literal rendering of Tinctoris' "Per A" than to spell out the full import: "Through all the terms beginning with the letter A."

The translation is rather heavily glossed with notes that offer a fuller explanation of the generally terse and laconic definitions of Tinctoris. In many cases these explanations have been supplied by reference to the fuller discussion of the particular topic given by Tinctoris himself in his later treatises or in contemporaneous works by other theorists. It has not been considered necessary to add a bibliography of works referred to in the notes; it should be noted, however, that the several references to Coussemaker concern only the work by him cited above. The notes are intended primarily for the aid of students entering upon the study of medieval and Renaissance music, as well as for the general historian who might be curious about the terminology and methods of musical thinking employed by the musicians of this period. Although the musicologist may not find much that is unknown to him in the notes, the Dictionary itself may be useful to him as a handy compendium for reference to the musical terms in use during a long period of Western music.

Due acknowledgment is hereby made to Dr. Frederick B. Crane for his reading of the manuscript of this book.

Carl Parrish

CONTENTS

TERMINORUM MUSICAE DIFFINITORIUM
(DICTIONARY OF MUSICAL TERMS)

Dedication :: 2

The Dictionary :: 6

Peroration :: 74

Additional Entries in the Brussels and
Bologna Manuscripts of the Dictionary :: 76

NOTES :: 79

BIBLIOGRAPHY :: 99

THE PRINTING OF TINCTORIS' DICTIONARY :: 101
    James B. Coover

XI

TERMINORVM
MVSICÆ
DIFFINITORIVM ::

Ioannis Tinctoris: Ad Illustrissimam
Virginem et Dominam
D. Beatricem de Aragonia:
Diffinitorium Musicae
Foeliciter Incipit

Prudentissimae virgini ac illustrissimae dominae D. Beatrici de Aragonia: Serenissimi principis divi Ferdinandi dei gratia regis Siciliae hierusalem et Hungariae probissimae filiae: Ioannes Tintoris: eorum qui Musicam profitentur infimus voluntariam ac perpetuam servitutem.

Moris est cuiuslibet scienciae praeceptoribus inclita virgo: dum ingeniorum suorum exercitia litteris mandant: aut ea viris illustribus: aut claris dirigere mulieribus. Cuius profecto motivum arbitror: vel ut eorum opera maiorem habeant auctoritatem, vel ut ipsorum animos: qui multum illis prodesse possunt (quod proprium virtutis est) sibi concilient. Ego autem enitens tuam (non adolescentulorum more, sed stabilitate et constantia) benivolentiam captare: tibi semper et prae omnibus morem gerere cupio. Quod mihi profuturum haud modicum expecto: si tibi ipsa persuadeas ei plurimum debere: a quo plurimum diligeris.

Quamobrem artis liberalissimae ac inter mathematicas honestissimae: videlicet divinae musicae studiosus: nunc a substantia, nunc ab accidenti suos diffinire terminos utilissimum existimans: quibus intellectis de ea acturi facilius et naturam eius et suarum partium comprehendant, praesens opusculum quod rationabiliter diffinitorium musicae dicetur, ad honorem tuae celsitudinis aedidi, aeditumque tibi mulierum clarissimae dirigendum censui, confidens id pergratum fore tibi: quae a poematibus oratoriis muneribus et aliis artibus bonis in quibus quod pulcherrimum excellis prudentissime secedens animi recreandi contemplatione ad hanc artem iocundissimam te confers non modo deductionem in omni suo genere per alios more principum Persarum atque medorum, sed etiam per teipsam assumens.

2

The Dictionary of Music of Johannis Tinctoris,
[being dedicated] to
The Most Illustrious Maid and Lady,
Princess Beatrice of Aragon,
Begins Auspiciously

To the very learned maid and most illustrious lady, Princess
Beatrice of Aragon, the very virtuous daughter of His Serene
Highness, the exalted Ferdinand, King of Sicily, Jerusalem, and
Hungary, by the grace of God, Johannes Tinctoris, the humblest
of those who profess music, gives willing and continual service.

It is the custom for the teachers of any science, renowned
maid, when they commit in writing the practice of their talents,
to dedicate them to exalted men or illustrious women. I consider
the reason for this to be either that their works may have a
greater authority, or that they may win for themselves the favor
of those who can be of much use to them (because it is a thing
of value). But I, seeking to win your good will (not in the manner of the young, but in steadfastness and perseverance), desire
always and before all things to please you. Therefore I should
expect no little profit for myself if you were to be convinced
that you are under the greatest obligation to the one by whom
you are most greatly loved.

Wherefore, being a student of the most liberal art, and the
noblest among the mathematical arts, namely divine music, and
believing it very useful to define its terms both in principle and
in detail, by which the things concerning it being understood,
those who practice it may the more readily grasp its nature and
its particulars, I have published the present little book, which
is called with reason a dictionary of music. And I have resolved
to dedicate the publication to the honor of Your Highness, the
most illustrious of women, believing that it will be pleasing to
you who, wisely withdrawing in contemplation for the refreshing
of your spirit from poetry, rhetoric, and the other worthy arts

Quo praestantissimum accedit nostrae facultatis decus, si quam formosissimam quam illustrissimam quam fontibus honesti habundantissime· refectam: quam denique omnium dominarum et suae aetatis et praeteritorum et futurorum temporum ab omni parte beatissimam cuncti praedicant ei studere dignatur.

Atqui regia proles si in ipso opusculo aliquid imperfectum quod te quam perfectissimam audeo dicere non deceat tui perspectissimi viderint oculi: parce precor. Nam (ut praeclare Virgilius cecinit) Non omnia possumus omnes. Unde quum diversis naturaliter gaudens: non unica arte contentus, plurium cognitionem attingere sicut et iam discretio novit: in dies animo ferventi praetendam, non mirum si in qualibet adeo perfectus non evadam: ut illos qui singulariter in singulis artibus operam et curam efficacissime ponunt: vincere possim. Tamen si in theorica musices pariter et praxi omnes nostri temporis cantores excedam aut excedar ab aliquo: tuae caeterorumque in ipsa arte peritissimorum perspicientiae discutiendum relinquo. Seipsum etenim (ut prudentibus placet) laudare vani est vituperare stulti.

in which you most gloriously excel, devote yourself to that most delightful art, making judgment upon its every species, not merely through others, like the Kings of the Medes and the Persians, but also by yourself. Thereby the grace of our knowledge is most excellently increased, if she whom all acclaim as the most beautiful, the most glorious, the most bountifully nourished at the sources of nobility, in short, as the most blessed of all ladies of her own time and of all times past and future, deems it worthy of her study.

However, royal child, if in this little work your own most perceptive eyes may see something imperfect which is not seemly to you, whom I dare to call the most perfect, be forbearing, I pray. For (as Virgil clearly stated) we cannot all do everything. Hence, since by nature I take pleasure in attaining knowledge in various subjects, not being content with a single art, as your discernment has already recognized, it is no wonder if I prove not to be perfect to such a degree that I should excel those who most effectively put energy and devotion on one particular art. Nevertheless, whether in musical practice and likewise in musical theory I may surpass all musicians of our time or be surpassed by some, I leave to the perspicacity of yourself and of others skilled in this art to determine. For (as the wise agree) to praise one's self is vain, to blame one's self is foolish.

Diffinitiones Terminorum Musicalium

: : : :

ET PRIMO PER A
INCIPIENTUM .. CAPITULUM I

A est clavis locorum are et utriusque alamire.

Acutae claves acuta loca et acutae voces sunt illae et illa quae in
manu ab alamire inferiori inclusive et usque ad alamire superius exclusive continentur.

Alamire est locus cuius clavis est a, et in qua tres voces, scilicet la
mi et re canuntur. Et ipsum est duplex, acutum et superacutum.

Alamire acutum est linea cuius clavis est a, et in qua tres voces,
scilicet la mi et re cantantur, la per naturam ex loco cfaut, mi
per bmolle ex loco ffaut gravi, et re per bdurum ex loco gsolreut gravi.

Alamire superacutum est spacium cuius clavis est a, et in quo tres
voces, la mi et re cantantur, la per naturam ex loco csolfaut,
mi per bmolle ex loco ffaut acuto, et re per bdurum ex loco
gsolreut acuto.

Alteratio est proprii valoris alicuius notae duplicatio.

Ambitus est toni debitus ascensus et descensus.

Definitions of Musical Terms

: : : :

AND FIRST THROUGH A,
THE BEGINNING, : : CHAPTER I

A is the letter-name of the degree a *re* [A] and both degrees of a *la mi re* [a and a'].[1]

Mean letter-names, mean degrees and mean syllables are those comprised in the [Guidonian] hand from the lower to the higher a *la mi re* [a to a'], including the former but not the latter.[2]

A *la mi re* is the degree whose letter-name is a, and on which three syllables are sung, namely *la, mi,* and *re.* It occurs in two ranges, mean and high [a and a'].

Mean a *la mi re* [a] is the line of the staff whose letter-name is a, and on which three syllables are sung, namely *la, mi,* and *re; la* in the natural hexachord beginning on the degree c *fa ut* [c], *mi* in the soft hexachord beginning on the degree low f *fa ut* [f], and *re* in the hard hexachord beginning on the degree low g *sol re ut* [g].

High a *la mi, re* [a'] is the space of the staff whose letter-name is a, and in which three syllables are sung, *la, mi, and re; la* in the natural hexachord beginning on the degree c *sol fa ut* [c'], *mi* in the soft hexachord beginning on the degree mean f *fa ut* [f'], and *re* in the hard hexachord beginning on the degree mean g *sol re ut* [g'].

Alteration is the doubling of the proper value of any note.[3]

Ambitus is the due range in the ascending and descending of a mode.[4]

7

Apothome est maior pars toni, quae semitonium maius vulgariter dicitur.

Are est spacium cuius clavis est a, et in quo unica vox, scilicet re canitur per bdurum ex loco Γut.

Armonia est amenitas quaedam ex convenienti sono causata.

Arsis est vocum elevatio.

Augmentatio est ad aliquam notam dimidiae partis sui valoris proprii additio.

Apotome is the larger part of a tone, which is commonly called the "larger" semitone.[5]

A *re* is the space of the staff whose letter-name is A, and in which only one syllable is sung, namely *re,* in the hard hexachord beginning on the degree Gamma *ut* [G].

Harmony is a certain pleasantness caused by an agreeable sound.[6]

Arsis is a rising of the syllables [in pitch].[7]

Augmentation is the addition to any note of half its own value.[8]

PER B CAPITULUM SECUNDUM

B est clavis locorum bmi et utriusque bfabmi. Et est duplex, videlicet quadrum et rotundum.

B quadrum est clavis locorum bmi et utriusque bfabmi, designans ibi per bquadrum mi canendum esse.

B rotundum est clavis utriusque bfabmi, designans ibi per bmolle fa canendum esse.

Bdurum est proprietas per quam in omni loco cuius clavis est g, ut canitur, et ex illo caeterae voces deducuntur.

Bfabmi est locus cuius una clavis est b rotundum, altera b quadrum, et in quo duae voces, scilicet fa et mi canuntur. Et est duplex, scilicet acutum et superacutum.

Bfabmi acutum est spacium cuius una clavis est b rotundum, altera bquadrum, et in quo duae voces, scilicet fa et mi canuntur, fa per bmolle ex loco ffaut gravi, et mi per bdurum ex loco gsolreut gravi.

Bfabmi superacutum est linea cuius una clavis est b rotundum, altera bquadrum. Et in qua duae voces, scilicet fa et mi canuntur, fa per bmolle ex loco ffaut, et mi per bdurum ex loco gsolreut acuto.

Bmi est linea cuius clavis bquadrum est, et in qua mi canitur per b bdurum ex loco Гut.

Brevis est nota in tempore perfecto valoris trium semibrevium. Et in imperfecto duarum.

B is the letter-name of the degree B *mi* [B] and of the two degrees of b *fa* b *mi* [b and b'] and is twofold, namely b natural or b flat.[9]

B natural is the letter-name of the degree B *mi* [B] and of the two degrees of b *fa* b *mi* [b and b'], indicating by b natural that *mi* is to be sung in those places.

B flat is the letter-name of the two degrees of b *fa* b *mi* [b and b'], indicating by b flat that *fa* is to be sung in those places.

The hard hexachord is that in which *ut* is sung on every degree of the staff whose letter-name is g, and from which the other syllables are reckoned.[10]

B *fa* b *mi* is the degree of the staff on which one letter-name is b flat and another b natural, and on which two syllables are sung, namely *fa* and *mi*. It occurs in two ranges, namely mean and high [b and b'].

Mean b *fa* b *mi* [b] is the space of the staff in which one letter-name is b flat, the other b natural, and on which two syllables are sung, namely *fa* and *mi; fa* in the soft hexachord beginning on the degree low f *fa ut* [f], and *mi* in the hard hexachord beginning on the degree low g *sol re ut* [g].

High b *fa* b *mi* [b'] is the line of the staff on which one letter-name is b flat and the other b natural, and on which two syllables are sung, namely *fa* and *mi; fa* in the soft hexachord beginning on the degree [mean] f *fa ut* [f'], and *mi* in the hard hexachord beginning on the degree mean g *sol re ut* [g'].

B *mi* is the line of the staff whose letter-name is b natural, and on which *mi* is sung in the hard hexachord beginning on the degree Gamma *ut* [G].

The breve is a note with the value of three semibreves in perfect time, and two in imperfect.[11]

PER C CAPITULUM TERCIUM

C est clavis locorum cfaut, csolfaut, et csolfa.

Canon est regula voluntatem compositoris sub obscuritate quadam ostendens.

Cantilena est cantus parvus, cui verba cuiuslibet materiae sed frequentius amatoriae supponuntur.

Cantor est qui cantum voce modulatur.

Cantus est multitudo ex unisonis constituta, qui aut simplex aut compositus est.

Cantus simplex est ille qui sine ulla relatione simpliciter constituitur, et hic est planus aut figuratus.

Cantus simplex planus est qui simplicibus notis incerti valoris simpliciter est constitutus, cuiusmodi est gregorianus.

Cantus simplex figuratus est qui figuris notarum certi valoris simpliciter efficitur.

Cantus compositus est ille qui per relationem notarum unius partis ad alteram multipliciter est aeditus, qui refacta vulgariter appellatur.

Cantus per medium est ille in quo duae notae sicut per proportionem duplam uni commensurantur.

Cantus ut iacet dicitur qui plane sine ulla diminutione canitur.

Cfaut est spacium cuius clavis est c, et in quo duae voces, scilicet fa et ut canuntur, fa per bdurum ex loco Γut, et ut per naturam ex loco proprio.

C is the letter-name of the degrees c *fa ut* [c], c *sol fa ut* [c'], and c *sol fa* [c''].

A canon is a rule showing the purpose of the composer behind a certain obscurity.[12]

A cantilena is a small piece which is set to a text on any kind of subject, but more often to an amatory one.

A cantor is one who performs a piece vocally.

Music is made up of a large number of individual sounds, and is either a single melody or a part-song.

A single melody is one composed without any accompanying part, and it is either plain or figural.[13]

A single melody in plain notes is one which is made up of notes of indefinite value, like Gregorian chant.

A single melody in figural notes is one composed with notes of definite value.

A part-song is one which is produced by the relationship of the notes of one part to those of another in various ways, and which is commonly called "composed" [i.e., fully written out].[14]

A *cantus per medium* is a piece in which two notes are measured as one, as in double proportion.[15]

A *cantus ut jacet* ["the piece as it lies"] is a piece which is sung entirely as it is written, without any diminution.

C *fa ut* [C] is the space on the staff whose letter-name is c, and in which two syllables are sung, namely *fa* and *ut; fa* in the hard hexachord beginning on the degree Gamma *ut* [G], and *ut* in the natural hexachord beginning on that very degree [C].

13

Circulus est signum quantitatis temporalis, qui aut perfectus aut imperfectus est.

Circulus perfectus est signum temporis perfecti.

Circulus imperfectus est signum temporis imperfecti, qui ab aliquibus semicirculus dicitur.

Clavis est signum loci lineae vel spacii.

Clausula est cuiuslibet partis cantus particula, in fine cuius vel quies generalis vel perfectio reperitur.

Color est idemtitas particularum in una et eadem parte cantus existentium quoad formam et valorem notarum et pausarum suarum.

Coma est illud in quo tonus superat duo semitonia minora.

Compositor est alicuius novi cantus aeditor.

Concordantia est sonorum diversorum mixtura dulciter auribus conveniens. Et haec aut perfecta aut imperfecta est.

Concordantia perfecta est quae continue pluries ascendendo vel descendendo fieri non potest, ut unisonus diapenthe, sub et supra quantum vis diapason.

Concordantia imperfecta est quae continue pluries ascendendo vel descendendo fieri potest, ut dytonus semidytonus diapenthe cum tono et diapenthe cum semitonio, sub et supra quantum vis diapason.

Coniuncta est dum fit de tono regulari semitonium irregulare aut de semitonio regulari tonus irregularis. Vel sic.

Coniuncta est appositio b rotundi aut bquadri in loco irregulari.

The circle is a representation of the mensuration of time, which is either perfect or imperfect.[16]

The whole circle is the representation of perfect time.

The incomplete circle, called the "semicircle" by some, is the representation of imperfect time.

A letter-name is the indication of the degree on the staff of a line or space.

A clausula is a small part of some section of a piece, at the end of which there is found either a pause or else the end of the piece.[17]

A *color* is the repetition of existing melodic segments in one and the same voice of a part-song, as to the shape and value of the notes and their rests.[18]

A comma is that interval by which a tone exceeds two lesser semitones.[19]

A composer is the creator of some new piece.

A consonance is a blending of different pitches which strikes pleasantly on the ear, and which is either perfect or imperfect.

A perfect consonance is one that cannot occur many times successively in ascending or descending above or below [a given note within] any number of octaves, such as the unison and fifth.[20]

An imperfect consonance is one that can occur several times successively in ascending or descending above or below [a given note within] any number of octaves, such as the major third, minor third, major sixth, and minor sixth.

A chromatic alteration occurs when a note that is normally a whole step is made an exceptional half step, or a note that is normally a half step is made an exceptional whole step, or else:[21]

A chromatic alteration is the placing of a flat or natural sign on an unaccustomed degree.

15

Coniunctio est unius vocis post aliam continua iunctio.

Contrapunctus est cantus per positionem unius vocis contra aliam punctuatim effectus. Et hic duplex, scilicet simplex et diminutus.

Contrapunctus simplex est dum nota vocis quae contra aliam ponitur est eiusdem valoris cum illa.

Contrapunctus diminutus est dum plures notae contra unam per proportionem aequalitatis aut inaequalitatis ponuntur, qui a quibusdam floridus nominatur.

Contratenor est pars illa cantus compositi quae principaliter contra tenorem facta inferior est supremo, altior autem aut aequalis aut etiam ipso tenore inferior.

Contratenorista est ille qui contratenorem canit.

Csolfa est spacium cuius clavis est c, et in quo duae voces, scilicet sol et fa canuntur, sol per bmolle ex loco ffaut acuto, et fa per bdurum ex loco gsolreut acuto.

Csolfaut est linea cuius clavis est c, et in qua tres voces, scilicet sol fa et ut canuntur, sol per bmolle ex loco ffaut gravi, fa per bdurum ex loco gsolreut gravi, et ut per naturam ex loco proprio.

A melodic interval is the immediate connection of one syllable after another.

Counterpoint is music made by setting the notes of one voice against those of another, and there are two kinds, namely simple counterpoint and counterpoint in diminution [i.e., florid].

Simple counterpoint is that in which a note of one voice is put against a note of another voice of the same time value.

Counterpoint in diminution is that in which several notes are put against one in equal or unequal proportion, which is called "florid" by some.[22]

The contratenor is that voice of a part-song, mainly written opposite the tenor, which is lower than the highest voice, but higher, or on the same level, or even lower than the tenor.[23]

A countertenor is one who sings the contratenor part.

C *sol fa* [c"] is the space of the staff whose letter-name is c, and in which two syllables are sung, namely *sol* and *fa; sol* in the soft hexachord beginning on the degree mean f *fa ut* [f'], and *fa* in the hard hexachord beginning on the degree mean g *sol re ut* [g'].

C *sol fa ut* [c'] is the line of the staff whose letter-name is c, and on which three syllables, namely *sol, fa,* and *ut* are sung; *sol* in the soft hexachord beginning on the degree low f *fa ut* [f], *fa* in the hard hexachord beginning on the degree low g *sol re ut* [g], and *ut* in the natural hexachord beginning on that very degree.

PER D CAPITULUM QUARTUM

D est clavis locorum dsolre dlasolre et dlasol.

Deductio est vocum de uno loco ad alium per aliquam proprietatem ordinatam ductio.

Diapason equivocum est ad tria, nam concordantiam coniunctionem et proportionem significat. Pro primo sic diffinitur.

Diapason est concordantia ex mixtura duarum vocum ab invicem perfecto diapenthe et diatessaron aut imperfecto diapenthe et tritono distantium effecta. Pro secundo sic.

Diapason est coniunctio ex distantia perfecti diapenthe et diatessaron, aut imperfecti diapenthe et tritono constituta. Pro tertio sic.

Diapason est proportio qua maior numerus ad minorem relatus, illum in se bis continet precise, ut duo ad unum et iiii ad ii. Et hic adverte quod quotienscumque diapason per se invenitur, de perfecto intelligitur. Est nam triplex, scilicet perfectum imperfectum et superfluum.

Diapason perfectum est illud quod constat ex quinque tonis et duobus semitonis, ut a mi de bmi usque ad mi de bfabmi acuto.

Diapason imperfectum est illud quod constat ex quatuor tonis et tribus semitonis, ut a mi de bmi usque ad fa de bfabmi acuto.

Diapason superfluum est illud quod constat ex sex tonis et uno semitonio minori, ut a fa de bfabmi acuto usque ad mi de bfabmi superacuto, et ista duo ultima discordantia sunt.

18

D is the letter-name of the degrees d *sol re* [d], d *la sol re* [d'], and d *la sol* [d"].

Deductio is the conduct of the syllables from one degree to another, through some particular hexachord.[24]

The word "octave" has three different meanings, for it indicates a consonance, a melodic interval, and a proportion. The first of these is defined thus:

An octave is a consonance produced by the blending of two sounds distant from one another by a perfect fifth plus a perfect fourth, or an imperfect fifth plus the tritone. The second meaning is thus:

An octave is a melodic interval formed at the distance of a perfect fifth plus a perfect fourth, or an imperfect fifth plus the tritone. The third meaning is thus:

An octave is a proportion in which the larger number, compared to the smaller, contains the latter within itself exactly twice, as two to one, and four to two. And note this, that whenever an octave is seen by itself it is understood to be perfect, for these are three kinds of octaves, namely perfect, diminished, and augmented.[25]

A perfect octave consists of five whole steps and two half steps, as from the *mi* of [low] b *mi* [B natural] up to the *mi* of mean b *fa* b *mi* [b natural].

A diminished octave consists of four whole steps and three half steps, as from the *mi* of b *mi* [B natural] up to the *fa* of mean b *fa* b *mi* [b flat].

An augmented octave consists of six whole steps and one lesser half step, as from the *fa* of mean b *fa* b *mi* [b flat] up to the *mi* of high b *fa* b *mi* [b' natural]. These last two octaves [i.e., *imperfectum* and *superfluum*] are dissonances.

Diapenthe tria significat, scilicet concordantiam coniunctionem et proportionem. Pro primo autem significato sic diffinitur.

Diapenthe est concordantia ex mixtura duarum vocum ab invicem diatessaron et tono, aut tritono et semitonio distantium effecta. Pro secundo sic.

Diapenthe est coniunctio ex distantia diatessaron et toni, aut tritoni et semitonii constituta. Et pro tercio sic.

Diapenthe est proportio qua maior numerus ad minorem relatus, illum in se totum et insuper eius alteram partem aliquotam continet, ut sunt tria ad duo, sex ad quatuor. Nunc autem notandum est triplex esse diapenthe, scilicet perfectum imperfectum et superfluum.

Diapenthe perfectum est illud quod constat ex tribus tonis et uno semitonio, ut a mi de elami gravi usque ad mi de bfabmi acuto.

Diapenthe imperfectum est illud quod constat ex duobus tonis et duobus semitoniis, ut a mi de elami gravi usque ad fa de bfabmi acuto.

Diapenthe superfluum est illud quod constat ex tribus tonis et uno semitonio maiori, ut si fa in elami acuto fingatur, et contra hoc mi in bfabmi superacuto ponatur. Et haec duo ultima diapenthe sunt discordantia. Ubicunque vero diapenthe sine aliqua adiunctione ponitur, de perfecto intelligitur.

Diapenthe cum semitonio equivocatur ad duo. Nam et concordantiam et coniunctionem designat. Unde pro primo significato sic diffinitur.

Diapenthe cum semitonio est concordantia ex mixtura duarum vocum diapenthe et semitonio ab invicem distantium effecta. Et pro secundo sic.

Diapenthe cum semitonio est coniunctio ex distantia diapenthe et semitonii constituta.

The word "fifth" means three things, namely a consonance, a melodic interval, and a proportion. The first meaning is explained thus:

A fifth is a consonance produced by the blending of two sounds distant from one another by the interval of a fourth plus a whole step, or the tritone plus a half step. The second meaning is thus:

A fifth is a melodic interval formed at the distance of a fourth plus a whole step, or the tritone plus a half step. The third meaning is thus:

A fifth is a proportion in which the larger number, compared to the smaller, contains the latter within itself, and in addition an aliquot half part of the latter, as three to two, and six to four. It should be noted that there are three kinds of fifths, namely perfect, diminished and augmented.[26]

A perfect fifth consists of three whole steps and one half step, as from the *mi* of low e *la mi* [e] up to the *mi* of mean b *fa* b *mi* [b natural].

A diminished fifth consists of two whole steps and two half steps, as from the *mi* of low e *la mi* [e] up to the *fa* of mean b *fa* b *mi* [b flat].

An augmented fifth consists of three whole steps and one larger half step, as in the case of *fa* sounded on mean e *la mi* [i.e., e′ flat] and *mi* in high b *fa* b *mi* [b′ natural] set against it. These last two fifths [*imperfectum* and *superfluum*] are dissonances. Wherever the fifth occurs without anything added, it is understood as a perfect fifth.

The term "minor sixth" has a twofold meaning, for it indicates both a consonance and a melodic interval. Hence the first meaning is explained thus:

A minor sixth is a consonance produced by the blending of two sounds distant from one another by a fifth plus a semitone. The second meaning is defined thus:

A minor sixth is a melodic interval formed at the distance of a fifth plus a semitone.

21

Diapenthe cum tono duo significat, scilicet concordantiam et coniunctionem. Hinc pro primo significato sic diffinitur.

Diapenthe cum tono est concordantia ex mixtura duarum vocum diapenthe et tono distantium effecta. Et ita pro secundo sic.

Diapenthe cum tono est coniunctio ex distantia diapenthe et toni constituta.

Diapenthe cum semiditono pro duplici significato accipitur, scilicet pro discordantia et coniunctione. Unde pro primo sic diffiniendum est.

Diapenthe cum semiditono est discordantia ex mixtura duarum vocum ab invicem diapenthe et semiditono distantium effecta. Et pro secundo sic.

Diapenthe cum semiditono est coniunctio ex distantia diapenthe et semiditoni constituta.

Diapenthe cum ditono equivocum est ad duo, ad discordantiam scilicet et coniunctionem. Hinc pro primo significato sic diffinitur.

Diapenthe cum ditono est discordantia ex mixtura duarum vocum ab invicem diapenthe et ditono distantium effecta. Et pro secundo sic.

Diapenthe cum ditono est coniunctio ex distantia diapenthe et ditoni constituta.

Diaphonia idem est quod discordantia.

Diatessaron etiam tria habet significata, scilicet concordantiam coniunctionem et proportionem. Pro primo significato sic diffinitur.

Diatessaron est concordantia secundum quid ex mixtura duarum vocum ab invicem tono et semiditono vel econtra distantium effecta. Pro secundo sic.

Diatessaron est coniunctio ex distantia duorum tonorum cum semitono praeposito aut postposito vel intermisso constituta. Et pro tercio sic.

The term "major sixth" means two things, namely a consonance and a melodic interval. The first meaning is explained thus:

A major sixth is a consonance produced by the blending of two sounds distant from each other by the interval of a fifth and a whole step. The second meaning is explained thus:

A major sixth is a melodic interval formed at the distance of a fifth plus a whole step.

The term "minor seventh" is taken with a twofold meaning, namely as a dissonance and as a melodic interval. As to the first, it should be defined thus:

A minor seventh is a dissonance produced by the blending of two sounds distant from each other by the interval of a fifth plus a minor third. For the second meaning, thus:

A minor seventh is a melodic interval formed at the distance of a fifth plus a minor third.

The term "major seventh" is twofold, meaning both a dissonance and a melodic interval. The first is defined thus:

A major seventh is a dissonance produced by the combining of two sounds distant from each other by the interval of a fifth plus a major third. For the second meaning, thus:

A major seventh is a melodic interval formed at the distance of a fifth plus a major third.

Diaphony is the same as dissonance.[27]

The word "fourth" also has three meanings, namely those of a consonance, a melodic interval, and a proportion. The first meaning is defined thus:

A fourth is a consonance produced by the blending of two sounds distant from each other by the interval of a whole step plus a minor third, or the opposite. For the second meaning, thus:

A fourth is a melodic interval formed at the distance of two major seconds plus a minor second placed either before, or after, or in between them. For the third meaning, thus:

23

Diatessaron est proportio qua maior numerus ad minorem relatus, illum in se totum continet et eius insuper terciam partem aliquotam, ut iiii ad iii, et viii ad vi.

Diastema idem est quod coma.

Diesis est una pars toni in quinque divisi.

Diminutio est alicuius grossi cantus in minutum redactio.

Discantus est cantus ex diversis vocibus et notis certi valoris aeditus.

Discordantia est diversorum sonorum mixtura naturaliter aures offendens.

Ditonus aequivocum est ad duo, nam concordantiam et coniunctionem designat. Unde pro primo significato sic diffinitur.

Ditonus est concordia ex mixtura duarum vocum ab invicem duobus tonis distantium effecta. Et pro secundo sic diffinitur.

Ditonus est coniunctio ex duorum tonorum distantia constituta.

Divisio est unius aut plurium notarum ab illa seu ab illis cum qua vel cum quibus regulariter est annumeranda vel sunt annumerandae separatio.

Dlasol est linea cuius clavis est d, et in qua duae voces, scilicet la et sol canuntur, la per bmolle ex loco ffaut acuto, et sol per bdurum ex loco gsolreut acuto.

Dlasolre est spacium cuius clavis est d, et in quo tres voces, scilicet la sol et re canuntur, la per bmolle ex loco ffaut gravi, sol per bdurum ex loco gsolreut gravi, et re per naturam ex loco csolfaut.

A fourth is a proportion in which the larger number, compared to the smaller, contains all the latter within itself, and in addition an aliquot third part of the latter, as four to three, and eight to six.[28]

Diastema is the same as "comma."

Diesis is one part of a whole tone which has been divided into five parts.[29]

Diminution is the reduction of any large piece into a small one.[30]

A discant is a piece composed of different voices, and with notes of definite time-values.[31]

A dissonance is a combination of different sounds which by nature is displeasing to the ears.

The term "major third" stands for two things, for it indicates both a consonance and a melodic interval. The first of these is defined thus:

A major third is a consonance produced by the blending of two sounds distant from one another by two major seconds. The second meaning is defined thus:

A major third is a melodic interval formed at the distance of two major seconds.

Division is the separation of a note from one with which it would normally be counted, or of several notes from those with which they would usually be counted.[32]

D *la sol* [d″] is the line of the staff whose letter-name is d, and on which two syllables are sung, namely *la* and *sol; la* in the soft hexachord beginning on the degree mean f *fa ut* [f′], and *sol* in the hard hexachord beginning on the degree mean g *sol re ut* [g′].

D *la sol re* [d′] is the space of the staff whose letter-name is d, and in which three syllables are sung, namely *la, sol,* and *re; la* in the soft hexachord beginning on the degree low f *fa ut* [f], *sol* in the hard hexachord beginning on the degree low g *sol re ut* [g], and *re* in the natural hexachord beginning on the degree c *sol fa ut* [c′].

25

Dsolre est linea cuius clavis est d, et in qua duae voces, scilicet sol et re canuntur, sol per bdurum ex loco Γut, et re per naturam ex loco cfaut.

Duo est cantus duarum tantum partium relatione ad invicem compositus.

Dupla idem est quod diapason. Unde secundum tria eius significata instar diapason diffinitur.

Dupla sexquialtera est proportio qua maior numerus ad minorem relatus, illum in se bis continet, et eius insuper alteram partem aliquotam, ut v ad ii et x ad iiii.

Dupla superbipartiens est proportio qua maior numerus ad minorem relatus, illum in se bis continet et insuper eius duas partes aliquotas unam facientes aliquantam, ut viii ad tria, et xii ad v.

D *sol re* [d] is the line of the staff whose letter-name is d, and on which two syllables are sung, namely *sol* and *re; sol* in the hard hexachord beginning on the degree Gamma *ut* [G], and *re* in the natural hexachord beginning on the degree c *fa ut* [c].

A duo is a piece composed of only two parts, which are in relation to each other.

Dupla is the same as *diapason*. Hence it is explained in the same manner as the three definitions under *diapason*.[33]

Dupla sesquialtera is a proportion in which the larger number, in relation to the smaller, contains the latter twice within itself, and in addition an aliquot half part of the latter, as five to two, and ten to four.[34]

Dupla superbipartiens is a proportion in which the larger number, in relation to the smaller, contains the latter within itself twice, and in addition two aliquot parts of the latter, making one aliquant part, as eight to three, and twelve to five.[35]

PER E CAPITULUM V

E est clavis utriusque efami et ela.

Ela est spacium cuius clavis est e, et in quo unica vox, scilicet la canitur per bdurum ex loco gsolreut acuto.

Elami est locus cuius clavis est e, et in quo duae voces, scilicet la et mi canuntur. Et est duplex, gravis et acutum.

Elami grave est spacium cuius clavis est e, et in quo duae voces, scilicet la et mi canuntur, la per bdurum ex loco Γut, et mi per naturam ex loco cfaut.

Elami acutum est linea cuius clavis est e, et in qua duae voces, scilicet la et mi canuntur, la per bdurum ex loco gsolreut gravi, et mi per naturam ex loco csolfaut.

Emiola idem est quod diapenthe, unde sicut diapenthe secundum tria eius significata eam diffinies.

Epigdous tria significat, scilicet discordantiam coniuntionem et proportionem. Pro primo eius significato sic diffinitur.

Epygdous est discordantia ex mixtura duarum vocum, tono ab invicem distantium effecta. Pro secundo sic.

Epygdous est coniunctio ex distantia toni constituta. Et pro tercio sic.

Epygdous est proportio qua maior numerus ad minorem relatus,

E is the letter-name of both degrees of e *la mi* [e and e′] and also of e *la* [e″].

'E *la* [e″] is the space on the staff whose letter-name is e, and in which one syllable is sung, namely *la,* in the hard hexachord beginning on the degree mean g *sol re ut* [g′].

E *la mi* is the degree whose letter-name is e, and on which two syllables are sung, namely *la* and *mi*. It is found in two ranges, low and mean.

Low e *la mi* [e] is the space on the staff whose letter-name is e, and in which two syllables are sung, namely *la* and *mi;* *la* in the hard hexachord beginning on the degree Gamma *ut* [G], and *mi* in the natural hexachord beginning on the degree C *fa ut* [c].

Mean e *la mi* [e′] is the line on the staff whose letter-name is e, and on which two syllables are sung, namely *la* and *mi;* *la* in the hard hexachord beginning on the degree low g *sol re ut* [g], and *mi* in the natural hexachord beginning on the degree c *sol fa ut* [c].

Hemiola is the same as *diapenthe,* hence you will define it according to the three meanings of that word.[36]

Epogdous means three things, namely a dissonance, a melodic interval, and a proportion. The first of its meanings is defined thus:[37]

Epogdous is a dissonance produced by the combining of two tones distant from one another by a whole step. For the second meaning, thus:

Epogdous is a melodic interval formed at the distance of a whole step. For the third meaning, thus:

Epogdous is a proportion in which the larger number, in relation

illum in se totum continet et eius insuper octavam partem, ut sunt ix ad viii, et xviii ad xvi.

Epytritus idem est quod diatessaron. Hinc secundum tria eius significata, ut diatessaron diffinietur.

Eufonia idem est quod armonia.

Extractio est unius partis cantus ex aliquibus notis alterius confectio.

to the smaller, contains the latter in itself, and in addition the eighth part of the latter, as nine to eight, and eighteen to sixteen.

Epitritus is the same as *diatessaron,* hence it is defined according to the three meanings of that word.[38]

Euphony is the same as harmony.

An extraction is the making of one voice part of a composition from some notes of another composition.[39]

PER F CAPITULUM SEXTUM

F est clavis utriusque ffaut.

Fa est quarta vox distans a tercia semitonio, et a quinta tono.

Fa sol est mutatio quae fit in csolfaut et in csolfa, ad descendendum de bduro in bmolle.

Fa ut est mutatio quae fit in cfaut et in csolfaut, ad ascendendum a bduro in naturam, et in utroque ffaut ad ascendendum a natura in bmolle.

Ffaut est locus cuius clavis est fa, et in quo duae voces, scilicet fa et ut canuntur, et est duplex, scilicet grave et acutum.

Ffaut grave est linea cuius clavis est f, et in qua duae voces, scilicet fa et ut canuntur, fa per naturam ex loco cfaut, et ut per bmolle ex loco proprio.

Ffaut acutum est spacium cuius clavis est f, et in quo duae voces, scilicet fa et ut canuntur, fa per naturam ex loco csolfaut, et ut per bmolle ex loco proprio.

Ficta musica est cantus propter regularem manus traditionem aeditus.

Fuga est idemtitas partium cantus quo ad valorem nomen formam et interdum quo ad locum notarum et pausarum suarum.

F is the letter-name of both degrees of f *fa ut* [f and f'].

Fa is the fourth syllable of the hexachord, distant from the third [*mi*] by a half step, and from the fifth [*sol*] by a whole step.

Fa-sol is the mutation that is made on c *sol fa ut* [c'] and on c *sol fa* [c"] in order to descend from the hard to the soft hexachord.[40]

Fa-ut is the mutation that is made on c *fa ut* [c] and on c *sol fa ut* [c'] in order to ascend from the hard to the natural hexachord, and on both positions of f *fa ut* [f and f'] to ascend from the natural to the soft hexachord.[41]

F *fa ut* is the degree whose letter-name is f, and on which two syllables are sung, namely *fa* and *ut,* and it is in two ranges, namely low and mean [f and f'].

Low f *fa ut* [f] is the line of the staff whose letter-name is f, and on which two syllables are sung, namely *fa* and *ut; fa* in the natural hexachord beginning on the degree c *fa ut* [c], and *ut* through the soft hexachord from that very degree.

Mean f *fa ut* [f'] is the line of the staff whose letter-name is f, and on which two syllables are sung, namely *fa* and *ut; fa* in the natural hexachord beginning on the degree c *sol fa ut* [c'], and *ut* in the soft hexachord from that very degree.

Musica ficta is melody brought about by reason of the regular tradition of the [Guidonian] hand.[42]

Fugue is the likeness of the voice-parts in a composition as to the value, name, and shape of their notes and rests, and sometimes even to their degree on the staff.[43]

PER G CAPITULUM SEPTIMUM

G est clavis [Γ] ut.

G est clavis utriusque gsolreut.

Γut est linea cuius clavis est Γ, et in qua unica vox, scilicet ut per bdurum ex loco proprio canitur.

Graves claves gravia loca et graves voces sunt illae et illa quae in manu ab are inclusive usque ad alamire exclusive continentur.

Gravissimus locus est Γut, gravissimus clavis et gravissima vox illius.

Gsolreut est locus cuius clavis est g, et in quo tres voces, scilicet sol re ut canuntur. Quod quidem duplex est, scilicet grave et acutum.

Gsolreut grave est spacium cuius clavis est g, et in quo tres voces, scilicet sol re et ut canuntur: sol per naturam ex loco cfaut, re per bmolle ex loco ffaut gravi, et ut per bdurum ex loco proprio.

Gsolreut acutum est linea cuius clavis est g, et in qua tres voces, scilicet sol re et ut canuntur: sol per naturam ex loco csolfaut, re per bmolle ex loco ffaut acuto, et ut per bdurum ex loco gsolreut acuto.

G is the letter-name of Gamma *ut* [G].

G is the letter-name of the two degrees of g *sol re ut* [g and g'].

Gamma *ut* is the line whose letter-name is Gamma [G], and on which only one syllable is sung, namely *ut,* from that very degree through the hard hexachord.

Low letter-names, low degrees, and low syllables are those comprised in the gamut from, and including, a *re* [A] up to, but not including, a *la mi re* [a].

Gamma *ut* is the lowest degree, the lowest letter-name, and the lowest syllable of that letter.

G *sol re ut* is the degree whose letter-name is g, and on which three syllables are sung, namely *sol, re,* and *ut,* and which actually occurs twice, namely in both low and mean ranges.

Low g *sol re ut* [g] is the space on the staff whose letter-name is g, and in which three syllables are sung, namely *sol, re,* and *ut; sol* in the natural hexachord beginning on the degree c *fa ut* [c], *re* in the soft hexachord beginning on the degree low f *fa ut* [f], and *ut* in the hard hexachord from that very degree.

Mean g *sol re ut* [g'] is the line on the staff whose letter-name is g, and on which three syllables are sung, namely *sol, re,* and *ut; sol* in the natural hexachord beginning on the degree c *sol fa ut* [c'], *re* in the soft hexachord beginning on the degree mean f *fa ut* [f'], and *ut* in the hard hexachord beginning on the degree g *sol re ut* [g'].

PER H CAPITULUM OCTAVUM

Hymnus est laus dei cum cantico.

Hymnista est ille qui hymnos canit.

PER I CAPITULUM NONUM

Imperfectio est terciae partis valoris totius notae aut partim ipsius abstractio.

Instrumentum est corpus naturaliter aut artificialiter soni causativum.

Intonatio est debita cantus inchoatio.

Jubilus est cantus cum excellenti quadam leticia pronunciatus.

THROUGH H, CHAPTER VIII

A hymn is the praise of God in song.

A hymnist is one who sings hymns.

THROUGH I, CHAPTER IX

Imperfection is the reduction of the entire value of a note, or of part of that note, by a third.[44]

An instrument is a device for producing sound, either naturally or artificially.[45]

An intonation is the appropriate beginning of a chant.[46]

A *jubilus* is a melody delivered with a certain high exuberance.[47]

PER L CAPITULUM DECIMUM

La est sexta et ultima vox, tono distans a quinta.

La mi est mutatio quae fit in utroque elami, ad ascendendum a bduro in naturam, et in utroque alamire a natura in bmolle.

La re est mutatio quae fit in utroque alamire, ad ascendendum a natura in bdurum, et in dlasolre ad ascendendum a bmolli in naturam.

La sol est mutatio quae fit in dlasolre et in dlasol, ad ascendendum de bmolli in bdurum.

Ligatura est unius notae ad aliam iunctura.

Lima est minor pars toni, quam alii semitonium minus appellant.

Linea est locus tractu quodam designatus, quam alii regulam dicunt.

Locus est vocum situs.

Longa est nota in modo minori perfecto valoris trium brevium, in imperfecto duorum.

La is the sixth and last syllable of the hexachord, distant by a whole step from the fifth syllable [sol].

La-mi is the mutation which is made on both degrees of e *la mi* [e and e′], in order to ascend from the hard to the natural hexachord, and in both degrees of a *la mi re* [a and a′] to ascend from the natural to the soft hexachord.[48]

La-re is the mutation which is made on both degrees of a *la mi re* [a and a′], in order to ascend from the natural to the hard hexachord, and on d *la sol re* [d′] to ascend from the soft to the natural hexachord.[49]

La-sol is the mutation which is made on d *la sol re* [d′] and on d *la sol* [d″] in order to ascend from the soft to the hard hexachord.[50]

A ligature is the joining together of one note to another.[51]

A limma is the smaller part of a whole tone, which some call the "small" semitone.[52]

A line is a certain degree of the staff, drawn out by prolongation, which some call a "rule."[53]

A degree is the place on the staff of the syllables.

A long is a note of the value of three breves in the minor perfect mode, of two breves in the [minor] imperfect mode.

PER M CAPITULUM DECIMUM

Manus est brevis et utilis doctrina, ostendens compendiose deductiones vocum musicae.

Maxima est nota in modo maiori perfecto valoris trium longarum, et in imperfecto duarum.

Melodia idem est quod armonia.

Melos idem est quod armonia.

Melum idem est quod cantus.

Mensura est adaequatio vocum quantum ad pronunciationem.

Mi est tercia vox, tono distans a secunda, et semitonio a quarta.

Mi la est mutatio quae fit in utroque elami, ad descendendum de natura in bdurum, et in utroque alamire ad descendendum de bmolli in naturam.

Minima est nota valoris individui.

Mi re est mutatio quae fit in utroque alamire, ad ascendendum a bmolli in bdurum.

Missa est cantus magnus cui verba Kyrie, Et in terra, Patrem, Sanctus, et Agnus, et interdum caeterae partes a pluribus canendae supponuntur, quae ab aliis officium dicitur.

Modus est quantitas cantus ex certis longis maximam, aut brevibus longam respicientibus constituta. Est igitur duplex, scilicet maior et minor.

Modus maior est quantitas cantus ex certis longis maximam

The [Guidonian] hand is a brief and useful system showing in a concise manner the degrees of the syllables used in music.[55]

The maxim is a note with the value of three longs in the perfect major mode, and two in the imperfect.

Melody is the same as harmony.[56]

Melos is the same as harmony.[57]

Melum is the same as song.[58]

Measure is the correct division of the notes, as far as their delivery is concerned.[59]

Mi is the third syllable of the hexachord, distant from the second [re] by a whole step, and from the fourth [fa] by a half step.

Mi-la is the mutation which is made on both degrees of e *la mi* [e and e′], in order to descend from the natural to the hard hexachord, and in both degrees of a *la mi re* [a and a′] to descend from the soft to the natural hexachord.[60]

A minim is a note of indivisible value.[61]

Mi-re is the mutation which is made on both degrees of a *la mi re* [a and a′], in order to ascend from the soft to the hard hexachord.[62]

The Mass is a large composition for which the texts Kyrie, *Et in terra, Patrem,* Sanctus, and Agnus, and sometimes other parts, are set for singing by several voices. It is called the "Office" by some.[63]

Mode is the measuring of a melody, determined by considering the maxim to consist of a definite number of longs, or the long to consist of a certain number of breves. It is, accordingly, twofold, namely major and minor.[64]

The major mode is the measuring of a melody, determined by

respicientibus constituta, qui subdividitur. Nam alius est perfectus alius imperfectus.

Modus perfectus est dum tres longae pro una maxima numerantur.

Modus vero maior imperfectus est dum duae tantum longae pro una maxima numerantur.

Modus minor est quantitas cantus ex certis brevibus longam respicientibus constituta. Qui etiam subdividitur. Nam alius est modus minor perfectus, alius imperfectus.

Modus minor perfectus est dum tres breves pro una longa numerantur.

Modus minor imperfectus est dum duae tantummodo breves pro una longa numerantur.

Motetum est cantus mediocris, cui verba cuiusvis materiae sed frequentius divinae supponuntur.

Multiplex proportionum genus est quo maior numerus ad minorem relatus, illum in se plus quam semel continet, ut duo ad unum, tria ad i, quatuor ad unum.

Multiplex superparticulare proportionum genus est quo maior numerus ad minorem relatus, illum in se totum plusquam semel continet, et eius insuper unam partem aliquotam, ut v ad ii, vii ad iii, novem ad quatuor.

Multiplex superpartiens proportionum genus est quo maior numerus ad minorem relatus, illum in se plusquam semel continet, et eius insuper aliquas partes aliquotas, facientes tamen unam partem aliquantam, ut sunt octo ad tria, xi ad iiii, et xiiii ad v.

Musica est modulandi peritia cantu sonoque consistens. Et haec triplex est, scilicet Armonica, Organica, ac etiam Rithmica.

Musica armonica est illa quae per vocem practicatur humanam.

42

considering the maxim to consist of a certain number of longs, which is subdivided, for one is the perfect major mode, the other the imperfect.

The [major] mode is perfect when three longs are reckoned as the equivalent of a single maxim.[65]

The major mode is imperfect, however, when only two longs are reckoned as the equivalent of a single maxim.

The minor mode is the measuring of a melody, determined by considering the long to consist of a certain number of breves. It, too, is subdivided, for one is the perfect minor mode, the other the imperfect.

The minor mode is perfect when three breves are reckoned as the equivalent of one long.

The minor mode is imperfect when only two breves are reckoned as the equivalent of one long.

A motet is a composition of moderate length, to which words of any kind are set, but more often those of a sacred nature.

Multiplex proportion is the kind in which the larger number, in relation to the smaller, contains the latter within itself more than once, as two to one, three to one, and four to one.[66]

Multiplex superparticulare proportion is the kind in which the larger number, in relation to the smaller, contains all of the latter within itself more than once, and in addition one aliquot part, as five to two, seven to three, and nine to four.[67]

Multiplex superpartiens proportion is the kind in which the larger number, in relation to the smaller, contains the latter more than once within itself, and in addition some aliquot parts, [the latter] making, however, one aliquant part, as eight are to three, eleven to four, and fourteen to five.[68]

Music is that skill consisting of performance in singing and playing, and it is threefold, namely harmonic, organal, and rhythmical.[69]

Harmonic music is that which is performed by the human voice.

43

Musica organica est illa quae fit in instrumentis flatu sonum causantibus.

Musica rithmica est illa quae fit per instrumenta tactu sonum reddentia.

Musicus est qui perpensa ratione beneficio speculationis canendi officium assumit. Hinc differentiam inter musicum et cantorem quidam sub tali metrorum serie posuit. Versus:

Musicorum et cantorum magna est differentia.
Illi sciunt ipsi dicunt quae componit musica.
Et qui dicit quod non sapit reputatur bestia.

Mutatio est unius vocis in aliam variatio.

Organal music is that which is made by instruments which produce the sound by wind.

Rhythmical music is that which is made by instruments which render the sound by touch.

A musician is one who takes up the metier of singing, having observed its principles by means of study. Hence, someone has set down the difference between a musician and a singer in the following jingle:

> There is a big difference between musicians and singers.
> These know, those talk about, what music is.
> And he who doesn't know what he talks about is considered an animal.[70]

A mutation is the changing of one syllable into another.[71]

PER N CAPITULUM XII

Natura est proprietas per quam in omni loco cuius clavis est c, ut cantatur, et ex illo caeterae voces deducuntur.

Neoma est cantus fini verborum sine verbis annexus.

Nota est signum vocis certi vel incerti valoris.

PER O CAPITULUM XIII

Octava idem est quod diapason aut dupla coniunctio et concordantia. Unde secundum haec duo significata, eam ut diapason diffinies.

Officium idem est quod missa secundum hispalos.

THROUGH N, CHAPTER XII

The natural hexachord is that in which *ut* is sung on every degree of the staff whose letter-name is c, and from which the other syllables are reckoned.

A *neuma* is a melody without words, added to the end of [a melody with] words.[72]

A note is the symbol of a sound, and is of either definite or indefinite time value.[73]

THROUGH O, CHAPTER XIII

Octave is the same as *diapason,* or at least in the two meanings of the latter as "melodic interval" and as "consonance." Hence you will define it according to those two meanings of *diapason.*

Office is the same as Mass, according to the Spaniards.[74]

PER P CAPITULUM XIIII

Pausa est taciturnitatis signum, secundum quantitatem notae cui appropriatur fiendae.

Perfectio equivocum est ad duo. Nam notae in sua perfectione permanentiam, et totius cantus aut particularum ipsius conclusionem designat. Unde pro primo significato sic diffinitur.

Perfectio est qualiter nota maneat perfecta ostensio. Et pro secundo sic.

Perfectio est totius cantus aut particularum ipsius perfectionis cognitio.

Prolatio est quantitas cantus ex certis minimis semibrevem respicientibus constituta. Quae quidem duplex est, scilicet maior et minor.

Prolatio maior est dum in aliquo cantu tres minimae pro una semibrevi numerantur.

Prolatio minor est dum in aliquo cantu duae tantum minimae pro una semibrevi numerantur.

Pronunciatio est venusta vocis emissio.

Proportio est duorum numerorum ad invicem habitudo. Et haec est duplex, scilicet equalitatis et inequalitatis.

Proportio equalitatis est quae ex equalibus numeris conficitur, ut duo ad duo, iii ad iii, et iiii ad iiii.

Proporcio inequalitatis est quae ex inequalibus numeris fit, ut duo ad unum, iii ad duo, et caetera. Et hic adverte quod in praesenti diffinitorio genera proportionum cum quibusdam speciebus suis diffinivi. Si vero plures habere cupias, in nostro proportionali musices invenies illas.

A rest is a sign of silence, to be made according to the length of the note for which it stands.

Perfection is a word with two meanings, for it designates the duration of a single note in its own perfection, and the conclusion of a whole piece or of any of its sections. Hence for the first, the meaning is defined thus:[75]

Perfection is a manifestation that a note should remain perfect. For the second meaning, thus:

Perfection is the recognition of the completion of a whole piece, or of any of its sections.

Prolation is the measuring of a melody, determined by considering the semibreve to consist of a certain number of minims. It is, of course, twofold, namely major and minor.[76]

Prolation is major in any piece when three minims are reckoned as the equivalent of one semibreve.[77]

Prolation is minor in any piece when only two minims are reckoned as the equivalent of one semibreve.

Pronunciation is the elegant delivery of the voice.

Proportion is the relationship of two numbers, one to the other, and it is twofold, namely of equality or of inequality.

A proportion of equality is one which is effected by like numbers, as two to two, three to three, and four to four.

A proportion of inequality is one which is made up of unequal numbers, as two to one, three to two, and so on. And note this, that in the present dictionary I have explained the kinds of proportions with certain of their species; if, however, you wish to have more examples, you will find them in my *Proportionale musices.*[78]

Proprietas est propria quaedam vocum producendarum qualitas.

Punctus est signum augmentationis aut divisionis aut perfectionis. Et hoc si alicui notae adiungatur. Si vero in circulo aut semicirculo a parte dextra aperto ponatur, significat quod prolatio maior est. Et si in semicirculo ab inferiori parte aperto ponatur, moram generaliter fiendam in illa nota supra quam constituitur designat. Qui punctus organi vulgariter dicitur.

The hexachord is a certain special disposition in the conduct of the syllables.[79]

A dot, if it is added to any note, is a sign of either augmentation, division, or perfection. If, however, it is put in a circle, or in the semicircle which is open on the right side, it indicates that the prolation is major. If it is put in a semicircle which is open on the lower side, it signifies thus that at that note above which it is placed a pause is made in all voices; this is commonly called an "organ point."[80]

PER Q CAPITULUM XV

Quadrupla est proportio qua maior numerus ad minorem relatus, illum in se quater precise continet, ut iiii ad unum, et octo ad duo.

Quadrupla sexquialtera est proportio qua maior numerus ad minorem relatus, illum in se quater continet et eius insuper partem aliquotam, ut ix ad ii, et xviii ad iiii.

Quadrupla superbipartiens est proportio qua maior numerus ad minorem relatus, illum in se quater continet et eius insuper duas partes aliquotas, unam facientes aliquantam, ut xiiii ad tria, et xxii ad quinque.

Quantitas est secundum quam quantus sit cantus intelligitur.

Quarta idem est quod diatessaron coniunctio et concordantia. Hinc secundum haec duo significata sicut diatessaron diffinitur.

Quinta idem est quod diapenthe concordantiam et coniunctionem importans. Igitur sicut diapenthe quoad haec duo significata diffinietur.

Quadrupla is a proportion in which the larger number, compared to the smaller, contains the latter within itself exactly four times, as four to one, and eight to two.

Quadrupla sesquialtera is a proportion in which the larger number, compared to the smaller, contains the latter within itself four times, and in addition an aliquot part of the latter, as nine to two, and eighteen to four.[81]

Quadrupla superbipartiens is a proportion in which the larger number, compared to the smaller, contains the latter within itself four times, and in addition two aliquot parts of the latter, making one aliquant part, as fourteen to three, and twenty-two to five.

Quantity is that degree according to which the measuring of a melody is understood.[82]

A fourth is the same as *diatessaron* in its meaning both as "melodic interval" and as "consonance." Hence it is explained according to these two meanings as *diatessaron* is.

A fifth is the same as *diapenthe,* referring to both a melodic interval and a consonance. It would be explained therefore, even as those two meanings of *diapenthe.*

PER R CAPITULUM XVI

Re est secunda vox tono distans a prima, totidem vero a tercia.

Reductio est unius aut plurium notarum cum maioribus, quas imperficiunt aut cum sociis annumeratio.

Regula idem est quod linea.

Re la est mutatio quae fit in utroque alamire, ad descendendum de bduro in naturam, et in dlasolre ad descendendum de natura in bmolle.

Re mi est mutatio quae fit in utroque alamire, ad ascendendum de bquadro in bmolle.

Res facta idem est quod cantus compositus.

Re sol est mutatio quae fit in dsolre et in dlasolre, ad descendendum de natura in bdurum, et in utroque gsolreut ad descendendum de bmolli in naturam.

Resumptio est cantus finiti ut pertinet replicatio.

Re ut est mutatio quae fit in utroque gsolreut, ad ascendendum a bmolli in bdurum.

Re is the second syllable of the hexachord, distant from the first [*ut*] by a whole step, just the same distance, in fact, as from the third syllable [*mi*].

Reduction is the reckoning of one or more notes together with larger notes, which they [the smaller notes], or their equivalents in value, render imperfect.[83]

A rule is the same as a "line" of the staff.

Re-la is the mutation which is made on both positions of a *la mi re* [a and a′] in order to descend from the hard to the natural hexachord, and in d *la sol re* [d′] to descend from the natural to the soft hexachord.[84]

Re-mi is the mutation which is made on both positions of a *la mi re* [a and a′] in order to descend from the hard to the soft hexachord.[85]

A *res facta* is the same as a part-song.[86]

Re-sol is the mutation which is made on d *sol re* [d] and on d *la sol re* [d′] in order to descend from the natural to the hard hexachord, and on both positions of g *sol re ut* [g and g′] to descend from the soft to the natural hexachord.[87]

A resumption is the repetition of a completed composition at the appropriate place.[88]

Re-ut is the mutation which is made on both positions of g *sol re ut* [g and g′] in order to ascend from the soft to the hard hexachord.[89]

PER S CAPITULUM XVII

Secunda equivocatur ad duo, scilicet ad discordiam [sic] et coniunctionem. Unde pro primo significato sic diffinitur.

Secunda est discordantia ex mixtura duarum vocum, tono vel semitonio ab invicem distantium effecta. Et pro secundo sic.

Secunda est coniunctio ex distantia unius toni vel semitonii constituta.

Semibrevis est nota in prolatione maiori valoris trium minimarum, et in minori duarum.

Semitonium duo significat, scilicet discordantiam et coniunctionem. Hinc pro primo significato sic diffinitur.

Semitonium est discordantia ex mixtura duarum vocum, duabus aut tribus diesibus ab invicem distantium effecta. Et pro secundo sic.

Semitonium est coniunctio ex distantia duarum aut trium diesium constituta. Et ita collige duplex esse semitonium, scilicet maius et minus.

Semitonium maius est illud quod ex tribus diesibus constat, ut de mi in bfabmi usque ad fa in eodem loco, quod a pluribus apothome seu semitonium diatonicum appellatur.

Semitonium minus est illud quod ex duabus diesibus tantummodo constat, ut de mi in alamire usque ad fa in bfabmi, quod a Platone lima, ab aliis semitonium Enarmonicum appellatur. Est et aliud semitonium quod Cromaticum dicitur. Fit autem dum canendo aliqua vox ad pulcritudinem pronunciationis sustinetur. Quotienscumque vero semitonium per se scriptum invenitur aut dicitur, minus esse intelligitur.

The word "second" means two things, namely a dissonance and a melodic interval. As for the first meaning, it is defined thus:

A second is a dissonance produced by the combining of two tones, distant from one another by a whole- or half-step. For the second meaning, thus:

A second is a melodic interval formed at the distance of a single whole- or half-step.

A semibreve is a note with the value of three minims in major prolation, and two minims in minor prolation.

The word "semitone" means two things, namely a dissonance and a melodic interval. The first meaning, therefore, is defined thus:

A semitone is a dissonance produced by the combining of two tones, distant from each other by either two or three *dieses.* For the second meaning, thus:

A semitone is a melodic interval formed at the distance of either two or three *dieses.* So, consider the semitone to be twofold, namely the greater and the lesser.[90]

The greater semitone is that which consists of three *dieses,* as from *mi* in b *fa* b *mi* to *fa* on the same degree, which is called by many the *apothome,* or "diatonic semitone."[91]

The lesser semitone is that which consists of only two *dieses,* as from *mi* in a *la mi re* to *fa* in b *fa* b *mi,* which is called by Plato a *limma,* and by others the "enharmonic semitone." There is also another semitone which is called the "chromatic." It is used when, in singing, some note is raised for the purpose of a beautiful delivery. But whenever a semitone is found by itself, either written or sung, it is to be understood as the lesser semitone.[92]

Semiditonus est equivocum ad duo, scilicet ad concordantiam et coniunctionem. Unde pro primo significato sic diffinitur.

Semiditonus est concordantia ex mixtura duarum vocum tono et semitonio ab invicem distantium effecta. Et pro secundo sic.

Semiditonus est coniunctio ex distantia unius toni et semitonii constituta.

Semicirculus idem est quod circulus imperfectus.

Septima perfecta idem est quod diapenthe cum ditono.

Septima imperfecta idem est quod diapenthe cum semiditono.

Sexquialtera idem est quod diapenthe aut emiolia proportio. Unde secundum hoc significatum sicut illa diffinitur.

Sexquitercia idem est quod diatessaron aut epitritus proportio. Hinc instar ipsorum quoad id significatum diffinienda est.

Sexquiquarta est proportio qua maior numerus ad minorem relatus, illum in se totum continet et insuper eius quartam partem aliquotam, ut v ad iiii, x ad viii.

Sexta perfecta idem est quod diapenthe cum tono.

Sexta imperfecta idem est quod diapenthe cum semitonio.

Sincopa est alicuius notae interposita maiore per partes divisio.

Sol est quinta vox tono distans a quarta totidemque ab ultima.

Sol fa est mutatio quae fit in csolfaut et in csolfa, ad descendendum de bmolli in bdurum.

58

The term "minor third" means two things, namely a consonance and a melodic interval. As for the first meaning, it is defined thus:

A minor third is a consonance produced by the blending of two tones, distant from one another by a whole-step plus a half-step. For the second meaning, thus:

A minor third is a melodic interval formed at the distance of one whole-step plus a half-step.

A semicircle is the same as the incomplete circle [of imperfection].[93]

A major seventh is the same as the fifth plus the major third.

A minor seventh is the same as the fifth plus the minor third.

Sesquialtera is a proportion which is the same as *diapenthe* or *emiolia*. Hence it is explained according to this meaning [i.e., as a proportion], just as they are.[94]

Sesquitertia is the same proportion as *diatessaron* or *epitritus*. Hence its meaning should be defined the same way as theirs.[95]

Sesquiquarta is a proportion in which the larger number, compared to the smaller, contains all of the latter within itself, and in addition a fourth aliquot part of the latter, as five to four or ten to eight.[96]

A major sixth is the same as a fifth plus a whole-step.

A minor sixth is the same as a fifth plus a half-step.

A syncopation is a division of some note into [two] parts by an interposed larger note.[97]

Sol is the fifth syllable of the hexachord, a whole step distant from the fourth syllable [*fa*], just the same distance as it is from the last syllable [*la*].

Sol-fa is the mutation which is made on c *sol fa ut* [c′] and on c *sol fa* [c″], in order to descend from the soft to the hard hexachord.[98]

Solfisatio est cantando vocum per sua nomina expressio.

Sol la est mutatio quae fit in dlasolre et in dlasol, ad descendendum de bduro in bmolle.

Sol re est mutatio quae fit in dsolre et in dlasolre, ad descendendum de bduro in naturam, et in utroque gsolreut ad ascendendum a natura in bmolle.

Sol ut est mutatio quae fit in utroque gsolreut, ad ascendendum a natura in bdurum, et in csolfaut ad ascendendum de bmolli in naturam.

Sonitor est qui instrumento artificiali, sive organico sive rithmico musicam exercet.

Sonus est quicquid proprie et per se ab auditu percipitur.

Spacium est locus supra vel infra lineam relictus.

Stema est dimidium comatis.

Subdupla est proportio qua minor numerus ad maiorem relatus, in illo bis precise continetur, ut unum ad duo.

Submultiplex proportionum genus est quo minor numerus ad maiorem relatus, in illo multipliciter precise continetur ut unum ad duo, et i ad iii.

Superacuta loca et superacutae voces sunt illae et illa quae ab alamire superiori usque ad ela inclusive in manu continentur.

Superbipartiens est proportio qua maior numerus ad minorem relatus, illum in se totum continet et insuper duas eius partes aliquotas unam facientes aliquantam, ut v ad iii.

Superparticulare proportionum genus est quo maior numerus ad

Solmization is the pronouncing of the hexachord syllables in singing by their proper names.

Sol-la is the mutation which is made on d *la sol re* [d'] and on d *la sol* [d''], in order to descend from the hard to the soft hexachord.[99]

Sol-re is the mutation which is made on d *sol re* [d] and on d *la sol re* [d'], in order to descend from the hard to the natural hexachord, and in both positions of g *sol re ut* [g and g'], to ascend from the natural to the soft hexachord.[100]

Sol-ut is the mutation which is made on both degrees of g *sol re ut* [g and g'] in order to ascend from the natural to the hard hexachord, and on c *sol fa ut* [c'] to ascend from the soft to the natural hexachord.[101]

A player is one who performs music on an artificial instrument, whether it is organal [i.e., a wind instrument] or rhythmic [i.e., a stringed instrument].[45]

Sound is whatever is perceived, properly and by itself, by hearing.

A space is the place left above or below a line of the staff.

A *stema* is half of a comma.[102]

Subdupla is a proportion in which the smaller number, in relation to the larger, is contained in the latter exactly twice, as one to two.[103]

Submultiplex proportion is a kind in which the smaller number, compared to the larger, is contained in the latter by an exact multiple of itself, as one to two, and one to three.[104]

High degrees and high syllables are those contained in the gamut from high a *la mi re* [a'] up to and including e *la* [e''].[105]

Superbipartiens is a proportion in which the larger number, compared to the smaller, contains the latter wholly in itself, and in addition two of its aliquot parts, making one aliquant part, as five to three.[106]

Superparticulare is a kind of proportion in which the larger

minorem relatus, illum in se totum continet, et eius aliquam partem aliquotam, ut iii ad ii, et iiii ad iii.

Superpartiens proportionum genus est quo maior numerus ad minorem relatus, illum in se totum continet, et eius insuper aliquas partes aliquotas, unam facientes aliquantam, ut quinque ad tria, et vii ad v.

Suppositio est aliquorum corporum ut voces loco notarum significent introductio.

Supremum est illa pars cantus compositi quae altitudine caeteras excidit.

number, compared to the smaller, contains all of the latter within itself, and in addition some aliquot part, as three to two, and four to three.[107]

Superpartiens is a kind of proportion in which the larger number, compared to the smaller, contains all of the latter within itself, and in addition some aliquot parts, making one aliquant part, as five to three, and seven to five.[108]

Substitution is the introduction of some other signs to represent the syllables in place of notes.[109]

The *supremum* is that voice-part of a part-song which exceeds the others in height of pitch.[110]

PER T CAPITULUM XVIII

T est littera quae per se ad aliquam partem cantus posita, tenorem
institutione significat, quae quidem si prima sit mei cognominis, quod Tinctoris est: mihi non dedecori venit, quum
et nomen domini ineffabile Tetragramaton ab ea sumat exordium.

Talea est idemtitas particularum in una et eadem parte cantus
existentium quoad nomen locum et valorem notarum et
pausarum suarum.

Tempus est quantitas cantus ex certis semibrevibus brevem respicientibus constituta. Quod quidem duplex est, scilicet perfectum et imperfectum.

Tempus perfectum est dum in aliquo cantu tres semibreves pro
una brevi numerantur.

Tempus imperfectum est dum in aliquo cantu duae semibreves
tantum pro una brevi numerantur.

Tenor est cuiusque cantus compositi fundamentum relationis.

Tenorista est ille qui tenorem canit.

Tertia perfecta idem est quod ditonus.

Tertia imperfecta idem est quod semiditonus.

Tesis est vocum depositio.

Tonus equivocum est ad quatuor. Nam significat coniunctionem
discordantiam intonationem et tropum. Hinc pro primo significato sic diffinitur.

Tonus est coniunctio ex distantia quinque diesum constituta. Et
pro secundo sic.

T is the letter which, when placed by itself on a certain voice-part of a composition, customarily indicates the Tenor, and which, since it may be the first letter of my surname, which is Tinctoris, came to me not unbecomingly, as the Tetragrammaton —the ineffable name of the Lord—also takes its beginning from this letter.[111]

A *talea* is the repetition of segments existing in one and the same voice-part of a composition, even to the name of their pitches and the value of their notes and rests.[112]

Time is the measuring of a melody, determined by considering the breve to consist of a definite number of semibreves. It is, of course, twofold, namely perfect and imperfect.[113]

The time is perfect in any piece when three semibreves are reckoned as the equivalent of one breve.

The time is imperfect in any piece when only two semibreves are reckoned as the equivalent of one breve.

The tenor is the foundation for the relationship [of the various voice-parts] of any part-song.[114]

A tenor-singer is one who performs the tenor part.

The major third is the same as the *ditonus*.

The minor third is the same as the *semiditonus*.

Thesis is a falling of the syllables [in pitch].[115]

The word "tone" has four meanings, for it designates a melodic interval, a dissonance, an intonation, and a mode. As for the first meaning, it is explained thus:

A tone is a melodic interval formed at the distance of five *dieses*. For the second meaning, thus:[116]

Tonus est concordantia [sic] ex mixtura duarum vocum quinque diesibus ab invicem distantium effecta. Et pro tercio sic.

Tonus est cantus intonatio. Et pro quarto sic.

Tonus est tropus per quem omnis cantus debite componitur. Huius autem significati octo sunt toni.

Tonus primus est ille qui ex primis speciebus diapenthe et diatessaron formatus; potest a suo fine diapason ascendere ac ditonum descendere, qui ab antiquis auctenticus protus appellatus est.

Tonus secundus est ille qui ex primis speciebus diapenthe et diatessaron formatus; potest a suo fine diapenthe cum ditono aut cum semiditono ascendere, qui plagalis aut subiugalis aut collateralis auctentici Prothi ab antiquis dicitur.

Tonus tercius est ille qui ex secundis speciebus diapenthe et diatessaron formatus; potest a suo fine diapason ascendere, ac ditonum vel semiditonum descendere, qui ab antiquis auctenticus deuterus est appellatus.

Tonus quartus est ille qui ex secundis speciebus diapenthe ac diatessaron formatus; potest a suo fine diapenthe cum ditono aut semiditono ascendere, ac diatessaron descendere, qui plagalis aut subiugalis aut collateralis auctentici deuteri ab antiquis dicitur.

Tonus quintus est ille qui dicitur ex tercia aut quarta specie diapenthe et tercia specie diatessaron formatus, et potest a fine suo diapason ascendere, ac ditonum vel semiditonum descendere, qui ab antiquis auctenticus tritus dicitur.

Tonus sextus est ille qui ex tercia aut quarta specie diapenthe et tercia specie diatessaron formatus; potest a suo fine diapenthe cum ditono aut semiditono ascendere, ac diatessaron descendere, qui plagalis aut subiugalis aut collateralis auctentici Triti a musicis antiquis appellatus est.

Tonus septimus est qui ex quarta specie diapenthe et prima specie

A tone is a consonance produced by the combining of two sounds distant from one another by five *dieses*. For the third meaning, thus:[117]

A tone is the intonation of a chant. For the fourth meaning, thus:[118]

A tone is a mode in which every chant is duly composed. However, in this meaning there are eight modes.[119]

The first mode is that which is formed by the first species of the fifth plus [the first species of] the fourth. From its final it can ascend an octave and descend a major third. It was called the authentic *protus* mode by older musicians.[120]

The second mode is that which is formed by the first species of the fifth plus [the first species of] the fourth. From its final it can ascend a major or minor seventh. It is called by older musicians the plagal, or lower, or parallel mode of the authentic *protus*.

The third mode is that which is formed by the second species of the fifth plus [the second species of] the fourth. From its final it can ascend an octave and descend a major or minor third. It was called by older musicians the authentic *deuterus*.

The fourth mode is that which is formed by the second species of the fifth plus [the second species of] the fourth. From its final it can ascend a major or minor seventh, and descend a fourth. It is called by older musicians the plagal, or lower, or parallel mode of the authentic *deuterus*.

The fifth mode is that which is said to be formed by the third or the fourth species of the fifth, plus the third species of the fourth. From its final it can ascend an octave, and descend a major or minor third. It is called by older musicians the authentic *tritus*.

The sixth mode is that which is formed by the third or the fourth species of the fifth, plus the third species of the fourth. From its final it can ascend a major or minor seventh, and descend a fourth. It was called the plagal, or lower, or parallel mode of the authentic *tritus* by older musicians.

The seventh mode is that which is formed by the fourth species

diatessaron formatus; potest a suo fine diapason ascendere ac ditonum vel semiditonum descendere, qui ab auctoribus antiquis auctenticus Tetrardus est appellatus.

Tonus octavus est ille qui ex quarta specie diapenthe et prima specie diatessaron formatus; potest a suo fine diapenthe cum ditono aut cum semiditono ascendere, ac diatessaron descendere, qui plagalis aut subiugalis aut collateralis auctentici tetrardi ab antiquis dicitur.

Istorum autem tonorum alii sunt regulares, alii irregulares, alii mixti, alii commixti, alii perfecti, alii imperfecti, alii plusquamperfecti.

Tonus regularis est qui in loco sibi regulariter determinato finitur.

Tonus irregularis est qui in alio loco quam in illo qui sibi regulariter est determinatus finem accipit.

Locus autem regularis primi et secundi toni est dsolre.

Locus regularis tercii et quarti toni est elami grave.

Locus regularis quinti et sexti toni est ffaut grave.

Locus vero regularis septimi et octavi est gsolreut grave.

Caetera vero loca sunt irregularia.

Tonus mixtus est qui si auctenticus fuerit descensum sui plagalis; si vero plagalis, ascensum sui auctentici attingit.

Tonus commixtus est ille qui si auctenticus fuerit cum alio quam cum plagali suo. Si vero plagalis cum alio quam cum suo auctentico miscetur.

Tonus perfectus est qui perfecte suum implet ambitum.

Tonus imperfectus est cuius ambitus non est perfectus.

of the fifth and the first species of the fourth. From its final it can ascend an octave and descend a major or minor third. It was called by older authorities the authentic *tetrardus*.

The eighth mode is that which is formed by the fourth species of the fifth and the first species of the fourth. From its final it can ascend a major or minor seventh, and descend a fourth. It is called the plagal or parallel mode of the authentic *tetrardus* by older musicians.

Some of these modes, however, are regular, others irregular; some mixed, others combined; some perfect, some imperfect, and others pluperfect.

A regular mode is one which is ended on the degree normally prescribed for it.

An irregular mode is one which takes the final on another degree than that which is normally prescribed for it.[121]

> The degree of the [final of the] regular first and second mode is d *sol re* [d].

> The degree of the [final of the] regular third and fourth mode is low e *la mi* [e].

> The degree of the [final of the] regular fifth and sixth mode is low f *fa ut* [f].

> The degree of the [final of the] regular seventh and eighth mode, however, is g *sol re ut* [g].

> Other degrees [of the final], however, are irregular.

A mixed mode is one which, if it is authentic, touches the descending range of its own plagal mode; if it is plagal, however, it touches the ascending range of its own authentic mode.[122]

A combined mode is one which, if authentic, is joined with some other plagal mode than its own; if, however, it is plagal, it is joined with some other authentic mode than its own.[123]

A perfect mode is one which completely fills its range.

An imperfect mode is one whose range is not complete.

Tonus plusquamperfectus est qui ultra suum ambitum si auctenticus fuerit, ascendit. Si vero plagalis, descendit.

Tripla est proportio qua maior numerus ad minorem relatus, illum in se ter precise continet, ut tria ad i, et vi ad duo.

Triplum antiqui posuerunt partem illam compositi cantus quae superiori magis appropinquabat.

Tritonus duo significat, scilicet discordantiam et coniunctionem. Unde pro primo significato sic diffinitur.

Tritonus est discordantia ex mixtura duarum vocum tribus tonis ab invicem distantium effecta. Et pro secundo sic.

Tritonus est coniunctio ex distantia trium tonorum constituta.

A pluperfect mode is one which, if authentic, ascends beyond its own range; if, however, it is plagal, it descends [beyond its own range].[124]

Tripla is a proportion in which the larger number, compared to the smaller, contains the latter within itself exactly three times, as three to one, and six to two.[125]

The *triplum* is that voice of a part-song which older musicians set as the one which most nearly approached the uppermost voice.[126]

The word "tritone" signifies two things, namely a dissonance and a melodic interval. As to the first meaning, it is defined thus:

A tritone is a dissonance produced by a combining of two sounds distant from each other by three whole steps. And for the second meaning, thus:

A tritone is a melodic interval formed at the distance of three whole steps.

PER V CAPITULUM XVIIII

Unisonus duo habet significata, scilicet solum sonum et concordantiam. Hinc pro primo significato sic diffinitur.

Unisonus est elementum musicae. Namque ex unisonis cantus componitur omnis. Et tamen dicitur unisonus quasi unus sonus. Pro secundo sic diffinitur.

Unisonus est concordantia ex mixtura duarum vocum in uno et eodem loco positarum effecta, quem dicunt fontem et originem omnium concordantiarum. Et tunc dicitur unisonus quasi una id est simul sonans.

Vox est sonus naturaliter aut artificialiter prolatus.

Ut est prima vox tono distans a secunda.

Ut fa est mutatio quae fit in cfaut et in csolfaut ad descendendum de natura in bdurum, et in utroque ffaut ad descendendum de bmolli in naturam.

Ut re est mutatio quae fit in utroque gsolreut ad ascendendum a bduro in bmolle.

Ut sol est mutatio quae fit in utroque gsolreut ad descendendum de bduro in naturam, et in csolfaut ad descendendum de natura in bmolle.

FINIS

The word "unison" has two meanings, namely that of a single sound and of a consonance. The first meaning is explained thus:

The unison is a basic element of music, for every melody is composed of unisons, yet the one single sound is called a "unison." As for the second meaning, it is explained thus:

The unison is a consonance caused by the combining of two syllables placed on one and the same degree of the staff, which men call the source and origin of all consonances; consequently it is called "unison," from sounding together, that is, simultaneously.

A tone is a [musical] sound produced either naturally or artificially.[127]

Ut is the first syllable of the hexachord, distant by a whole step from the second syllable [*re*].

Ut-fa is the mutation which is made on c *fa ut* [c] and on c *sol fa ut* [c'] in order to descend from the natural to the hard hexachord, and on both degrees of f *fa ut* [f and f'] to descend from the soft to the natural hexachord.[128]

Ut-re is the mutation which is made on both degrees of g *sol re ut* [g and g'] in order to ascend from the hard to the soft hexachord.[129]

Ut-sol is the mutation which is made on both degrees of g *sol re ut* [g and g'] in order to descend from the hard to the natural hexachord, and on c *sol fa ut* [c'] to descend from the natural to the soft hexachord.[130]

THE END

Joannis Tinctoris ad
Divam Beatricen de Aragonia Peroratio

Hoc opusculum dei gratia solutum tibi gloriosissima Diva Beatrix tuus offert Joannes Tinctoris. Quod ut benigne suscipias: auctorique faveas humilime precatur. Qui non solum id: sed siqua alia animi corporis ac fortunae bona: si superorum dono collata sint: omnia tuo submittit imperio. Deum amplius exorans: ut talem qualem te fecit; caeterarum scilicet Dominarum perfectissimam perpetuo servare tuerique dignetur.

AMEN

Peroration of Johannes Tinctoris to
The Divine Beatrice of Aragon

This little work, finished by the grace of God, your Johannes Tinctoris offers you, most glorious, divine Beatrice. He begs humbly that you look kindly upon it, and be favorable to its author, who submits everything to your command, not only this, but whatever other good things of mind, body, and fortune that may be bestowed as a gift from above; praying God, moreover, that He may always deign to protect and keep you just what he made you: the most perfect of all ladies.

AMEN

Found only in the Brussels manuscript.

Carmen est quicquid cantari potest.

Diacisma est dimidium semitonii minoris.

Diesis secundum aliquos idem est quod semitonium minus, secundum alios ipsius semitonii minoris dimidium. Nonnulli vero diesim esse volunt quintam partem toni, alii tertiam, quartam et octavam. Atque si Thomae credamus diesis ipsa semitoniorum est differentia, sed quicquid sit ut philosophus asserit in Capitulo metaphesicae, diesis non secundum auditum sed secundum rationem distinguitur.

Intervallum est soni gravis et acuti distantia.

Scisma est dimidium comatis.

Symphonia idem est quod concordantia.

Found only in the Bologna manuscript.

B molle est proprietas per quam in omni loco cuius clavis est f, ut canitur, et ex illo ceterae voces deducuntur.

Numerus est aggregatio ex unitatibus existens.

Found only in the Brussels manuscript.

A song is anything which can be sung.

The *diacisma* is half of the lesser semitone.[131]

A *diesis,* according to some, is the same as the lesser semitone; according to others it is half of that lesser semitone. Some, however, hold it to be the fifth part of a tone, others the third, the fourth, or the eighth part. But, if we may believe Thomas, the *diesis* is the difference between the major and the minor semitones. Whatever the philosopher may say in his chapter on metaphysic, though, the *diesis* is not distinguished by hearing, but by [mathematical] calculation.[132]

An interval is the distance from a low to a high sound.

The *scisma* is half of a comma.[133]

Symphony is the same as consonance.

Found only in the Bologna manuscript.

The soft hexachord is that position of the hexachord in which *ut* is sung on every degree of the staff whose pitch is f, and from which the other syllables are reckoned.[134]

A number is a sum consisting of [a collection of] units.[135]

THE GAMUT

MODERN PITCH-DESIGNATIONS		HEXACHORDS						COMPOUND NAMES OF PITCH-DEGREES	RANGES
e″							la	e la	
d″						la	sol	d la sol	
c″						sol	fa	c sol fa	*Super-acutae*
b′						fa	mi	b fa (or) b mi	
a′					la	mi	re	a la mi re	
g′					sol	re	ut	g sol re ut	
f′					fa	ut		f fa ut	
e′				la	mi			e la mi	
d′			la	sol	re			d la sol re	*Acutae*
c′			sol	fa	ut			c sol fa ut	
b			fa	mi				b fa (or) b mi	
a		la	mi	re				a la mi re	
g		sol	re	ut				G sol re ut	
f		fa	ut					F fa ut	
e	la	mi						E la mi	
d	sol	re						D sol re	*Graves*
c	fa	ut						C fa ut	
B	mi							B mi	
A	re							A re	
G	ut							Γut	

NOTES

1. In the Dictionary, there is an entry such as this for each of the pitches, from the lowest (G) to the highest (e″), which made up the full range of notes—called the "gamut," from *Gamma* + *ut*—which was officially recognized by theory in Tinctoris' time (although in practice this range was sometimes exceeded at either end). The following remarks are intended as a general explanation covering all these entries.

On page 78, a diagram shows all the pitches included in the gamut. The manner in which they are entered in the Dictionary is seen in the column headed "Compound names of pitch-degrees," while their corresponding pitches in present-day terminology are seen in the column headed "Modern pitch-designations." (In the latter, middle c is designated as c′; in the translation of the Dictionary, the corresponding modern pitch-designation is added, between brackets, after each reference by Tinctoris to a pitch-degree.) Between these two columns, running vertically, are the hexachords included in the gamut.

The hexachord (Gr. "six-tone"), the scale of six diatonic notes on which medieval and Renaissance theory was based, existed in three different pitch-successions: those starting on c and c′ (the "natural" hexachord), f and f′ (the "soft"), and G, g, and g′ (the "hard"). In the Dictionary, the word "hexachord" itself is never used; the hard, soft, and natural hexachords are referred to as *b durum, b molle,* and *natura,* respectively. (See note 24.) All three had the same interval-pattern; the fact that the hexachord on F was the same in this respect as the others is explained by the twofold function of the pitch b, which was taken as either flat or natural, according to whether it was used in the soft or the hard hexachord.

Each compound name by which Tinctoris refers to the various pitch-degrees consists of a pitch-letter followed by the syllables for which that pitch can stand in each of the three hexachords. Thus, middle c (c′) is called c *sol fa ut* (usually written without spaces: "csolfaut"), since it can be *sol* in the soft hexachord, *fa* in the hard hexachord, and *ut* in the natural hexachord.

Six of the compound names occur twice in the same form in the gamut —e *la mi,* f *fa ut,* g *sol re ut,* a *la mi re,* b *fa,* and b *mi*—so that a differentiation for the purpose of indicating actual pitches is made by reference to three different octave ranges: low (*graves,* from A through g), mean (*acutae,* literally "high," from a through g′), and high (*superacutae,* literally "highest," from a′ through e″). The lowest note of the gamut was not included in this scheme of octave ranges, and was usually indicated by the Greek letter Γ, to distinguish it from the G an octave higher; the latter, like the pitches

79

below it, was written as a capital, while all pitches above it were indicated in lower case. In many Renaissance diagrams of the gamut, however, the uppermost five notes are indicated by double letters: aa, bb, etc.

2. The hand referred to here (. . . *in manu*) is the "Guidonian" hand which is briefly described in the entry *Manus* (q.v.). It was a system for learning and recalling the compound pitch-names used in the gamut, which were associated with various parts of the left hand. A diagram of the Guidonian hand appears in many early treatises on music, including Tinctoris' own *Expositio manus* ("Explanation of the hand"), which is printed in Coussemaker IV (the hand being on p. 3).

3. A characteristic feature of medieval and Renaissance notation in compositions with perfect mensuration (i.e., triple meter) is the use of two notes of the same shape to fill the time value normally occupied by three such notes, or their equivalent. When this occurred, the second of the two notes was "altered" as described in this entry, i.e., it was read as if it were twice its written value. Very often the necessity for alteration had to be deduced by the singer himself from the context of the music; if there were some doubt about it, the composer usually put a dot after the note in question. This was called the *punctus perfectionis* ("dot of perfection"), also the *punctus divisionis* ("dot of division"), which functioned much as a modern bar line. Such a dot had a different effect than the *punctus additionis* ("dot of addition") described in note 8. Tinctoris refers to these uses of the dot, as well as others, in the entry *Punctus* (q.v.).

4. See the entry *Tonus,* where Tinctoris explains the four different meanings of this word. As used here, it is the fourth of those meanings, i.e., it is a church mode, the range or compass of which is normally an octave. It is the *ambitus* which determines the authentic or plagal character of a mode; generally speaking, if the ambitus lies an octave above the final, the mode is authentic, but if it descends a fourth below and ascends a fifth above the final, the mode is plagal. (See note 120.)

5. In the Pythagorean system of tuning, a difference was made between the chromatic semitone from b flat to b (the *apothome,* or "greater semitone," equal to 114 cents) and the diatonic semitone from b to c, and from e to f (the *limma,* or "lesser semitone," equal to 90 cents). (See notes 91 and 92.)

6. The word "harmony" is used in the general meaning of an agreeable intervallic relationship of two or more notes, whether sounded successively (melodically) or simultaneously (harmonically). In this connection, see Tinctoris' definition of *Melodia*.

7. The terms *Arsis* and its antonym *Thesis* (q.v.) were sometimes used to refer to strong and weak accents, although the manner in which they are employed here by Tinctoris is that which is commonly found in other treatises. The verbal canon, *per arsin et thesin,* was often used to indicate melodic inversion, as of a cantus firmus.

8. Augmentation in reference to a single note, as in this entry, was in-

dicated in Tinctoris' time as it is today, by the use of a dot, called the *punctus augmentationis* or *punctus additionis* ("dot of augmentation," or "addition"), a feature of notation that is first mentioned in treatises of the fourteenth century. See note 3, also the entry *Punctus*.

9. As indicated in note 1, b was an ambiguous note in the gamut, and was sung as b natural when the performer thought of the music as being in the hard hexachord (hence as *mi*), but as b flat when thinking of it in the soft hexachord (hence as *fa*).

10. In the Bologna manuscript of the Dictionary, but not elsewhere, this entry is followed by a parallel description of the soft hexachord. (The latter is seen on p. 76, in the list of additional entries not in the original printed edition: *B molle est proprietas. . . .*) Bellermann called attention to the lack of an entry concerning the soft hexachord, and also to the fact that the third of the three different hexachords—the natural, starting on c—is defined in a parallel manner to that of *B durum* under the entry *Natura* (q.v.). It will be noted that *proprietas* has been translated as "hexachord"; for further explanation of this, see note 24.

11. The word "time" is used in the translation as one of the three common degrees of mensuration (i.e., time relationships), the other two being "mode" and "prolation." Mode refers to the division of the long into breves, time to the division of the breve into semibreves, and prolation to the division of semibreves into minims. In each of these degrees, the division could be perfect or imperfect, i.e., the long, breve, or semibreve could be divided into either three or two notes of the next smaller degree.

12. Tinctoris refers here to compositions which are notated incompletely or in a deliberately false manner (the "puzzle canon"), and to which a verbal canon (i.e., a rule or guide), couched in more or less cryptic terms, supplies a hidden clue to the proper manner of performance. Such canons occur quite frequently in the music of the latter fifteenth and early sixteenth centuries; an example by Dufay may be seen in Apel-Davison, *Historical Anthology of Music,* vol. I, no. 66c.

13. By "plain or figural," Tinctoris means that a melody might be either in notes of even but indefinite value, such as plainsong (see the entry *Cantus simplex planus*), or in precisely measured notes of varying time values. (In this entry, Coussemaker, after the Brussels manuscript, has the word *ratione* instead of *relatione*.)

14. In his *Liber de arte contrapuncti* (Coussemaker IV, p. 129), Tinctoris again states that *refacta* is written-out counterpoint, as compared to improvised counterpoint (called *super librum cantare*—i.e., "to sing upon the book"—in the same treatise). This interpretation of the word has been questioned by E. Ferand, however, who, in his article, "What is Res Facta?" (*Journal of the American Musicological Society,* Fall, 1957, p. 141), claims that *refacta* means "florid" as opposed to "simple" counterpoint. (The word itself is spelled *resfacta* in Coussemaker, and written as *Res facta* in a separate entry in Tinctoris' Dictionary, q.v.)

15. The use of the expression *per medium* to indicate the halving of note values in one of the voice parts of a polyphonic piece, while not common, does occur in certain fifteenth-century manuscripts. A notable example is in the verbal canon of the chanson *Se j'ay perdu*, of the Oxford manuscript Canonici 213, folio 114.

16. The circle referred to appeared at the beginning of the piece, and was the equivalent of a modern time signature representing perfect (triple) time, while the incomplete circle represented imperfect (duple) time, as stated in the next two entries. "Time" is used here as in note 11, i.e., it applies to the division of the breve.

17. In this definition, the word "clausula" (Lat. "close," "ending") has the meaning of a "cadence," either at the end of a piece or of any section of a piece. In the late twelfth and early thirteenth centuries, the word had a very different meaning, namely that of a polyphonic composition in which a melismatic passage of a chant was used as a cantus firmus to which one or two upper parts were composed.

18. The word "color" in this sense is most often used in reference to the cantus firmus tenors of motets, although it appears to have also a broader meaning which included any kind of borrowing or quotation from other compositions. (See note 112.) Still another meaning of the word *color* is that of a literal "coloring" of certain notes (making them red in the period of black notation, and black in the period of white notation, i.e. after c. 1450), which had the effect of shortening their values by a third; in other words, of making a normally perfect note imperfect. Tinctoris seems not to have used the word in this meaning, even though he has examples of coloration in his treatise on mensural notation, and explains them as one means of bringing about imperfection (Coussemaker IV, pp. 65-66).

19. The Pythagorean whole tone was equal to 204 cents. Since each "lesser" semitone was equal to 90 cents (see note 5), the difference between two lesser semitones and the whole tone was 24 cents, the "Pythagorean comma." (Tinctoris spells "comma" here, and elsewhere in the Dictionary, as "coma.")

20. This statement is explained by reference to the more complete exposition of the consonances in Tinctoris' counterpoint treatise (Coussemaker IV, p. 79). He says there that the perfect consonances are the unison, fourth, fifth, and octave; then the octave plus fourth, octave plus fifth, and double octave; then the double octave plus fourth, double octave plus fifth, and triple octave. (For an English rendering of this passage—in which the Latin names for the intervals are retained—see Albert Seay's translation of Tinctoris' *Liber de arte contrapuncti,* p. 20, American Institute of Musicology, 1961.) In the condensed explanation of the Dictionary, the fourth is only obliquely stated to be a perfect consonance through the phrase "above and below," i.e., a fifth below any given note is the fourth above the lower octave of that note. It is curious that Tinctoris should have described perfect consonances as those which "cannot occur many times successively . . ." and imperfect consonances (in the following

entry) as those which "can occur many times successively. . . ." Perhaps this is merely a circuitous way of saying that there are more imperfect than perfect consonances.

21. The modern equivalent of *coniuncta* is "chromatic alteration"; the latter word in this context refers to a pitch modification brought about by the use of an accidental, and is quite different in meaning from "alteration" as used in the entry *Alteratio* (q.v.), which refers to a rhythmic modification. The entry *Coniuncta* is of special interest in having been quoted by Ramos de Pareja in his *Musica practica,* Bologna, 1482 (modern edition, Johannes Wolf, *Musica practica Bartolomei Rami de Pareia.* Leipzig, 1901, p. 30), where Tinctoris is mentioned as authority for the statement. In the two *coniuncta* entries, Tinctoris may be referring to unwritten accidentals (*musica ficta*) in the first, and written ones in the second. In regard to written accidentals, the natural sign (*b quadri*), could mean a sharp as well as a natural.

22. For an explanation of the word "proportion" in this entry, see note 34, also the entry *Proportio.*

23. By "opposite," Tinctoris may refer to the position of the contratenor on the two facing pages of a choir book, where, in a part-composition, the contratenor part often appeared on the lower portion of the page to the right, opposite the tenor part on the lower portion of the page to the left. The rest of the sentence refers to the varying range of the contratenor part.

24. The word *deductio* is one not often found in early treatises, and seems to be used by Tinctoris as a sort of synonym for "hexachord," a word which he never uses, as was mentioned above. In place of it, he employs three other terms, each with a slightly different meaning: 1) *proprietas,* 2) *b durum* (also *b molle* and *natura,* see note 1), and 3) *deductio.* The distinction appears to be as follows:
    1) *proprietas* is the name for the particular arrangement of intervals in any hexachord, regardless of its position in the gamut;
    2) *b durum, b molle,* and *natura* are those beginning on g, f, and c respectively, regardless of the octave range in which each occurs;
    3) *deductio* is one particular hexachord in a particular range.
In his treatise on the hexachord system, *Expositio manus* (Coussemaker IV, p. 8), Tinctoris says that there are seven deductions: those on G, c, f, g, c', f', and g'. A somewhat similar use of the word *deductio* is found in the anonymous treatise, *Quatuor principalia,* c. 1380, formerly attributed to Simon Tunstede (Coussemaker IV, p. 219).

25. "Proportion" in this sense refers to an acoustical relationship of vibration frequencies, rather than to the proportions used in mensural notation (see note 34). The proportion (ratio) of two over one gives the interval of the octave. In his "third meaning of the word octave," then, Tinctoris is defining the vibration ratio of the two tones which produce this interval.

26. See note 25. The proportion of three over two gives the vibration-

ratio of the perfect fifth. An "aliquot" number is one which can divide a larger number without a remainder.

27. This is the Greek meaning of "diaphony" (cf. *symphonia*, "consonance"). The word *diaphonia* was also used by medieval theorists in reference to organum style. Cf. Tinctoris' definition of *Discantus*, a word which appears to be a Latin translation of the Greek word *diaphonia*, but which he uses with a very different meaning than that of "dissonance."

28. See notes 25 and 26. The proportion of four over three gives the interval of the perfect fourth.

29. This gives the figure of 41 cents, the *minor diesis*, a term used to define the difference between the octave and three major thirds, in just intonation, i.e., the system of tuning based on the true ratio of intervals. In Greek theory, the *diesis* was the quarter tone which occurred between b and c in the enharmonic genus of the tetrachord.

30. What is meant here is the performance of a piece in smaller note values than those in which it is actually written, i.e., in diminution. "Large" and "small" refer, therefore, to notes which would be "large" as written, but "small" as performed, if they were to be sung in diminution. The degree of diminution could vary (double, triple, etc.), and this was usually indicated by a proportional sign. See notes 15 and 34.

31. The definition seems to say that discant is simply a broad term for any kind of polyphonic composition, unless the word *certus* is used by Tinctoris in the sense of "fixed" in time values in all voices, i.e., in note-against-note style.

32. The "separation" mentioned in the definition was to insure the alteration of a note when necessary (see the entry *Alteratio*), which was indicated by the use of the dot as a sort of bar line (the *punctus divisionis*), explained in note 3.

33. Although the definition states that *dupla* and *diapason* were used synonymously, the latter was the common term for a proportion of pitch (see note 25), while the former was the usual designation for a proportion of time (see note 34).

34. The word "proportion," in medieval and Renaissance musical theory, was used both as a term of measurement of pitch intervals and of time durations. In the former sense, it is used in the Dictionary by Tinctoris to describe the relative vibration-ratios of the pair of tones which form the intervals of the octave, fifth, and fourth (see notes 25, 26, and 28). In the latter sense, it is used to define changes made in the time values in relation to their normal values. The simplest and most commonly occurring of such changes is that of halving the values, which has already been mentioned (see notes 15 and 30, and the entries to which they refer: *Cantus per medium* and *Diminutio*), and which is the equivalent of present-day *alla breve*, or "cut-time." But occasionally changes were introduced that were more complex, such as those referred to in this entry and

that which follows it. If the proportional change called *dupla sesquialtera* were introduced into a voice part (the symbol for such a change being the figure 5 over 2), the result would be that five notes thereafter would be equal in time value to two notes of the same shape before the point where the proportional change occurred.

35. The term "aliquot" is defined in note 26. "Aliquant" means a number which is contained in another number, but which cannot divide it without a remainder. When the proportional change called *dupla superbipartiens* was introduced (its symbol being the figure 8 over 3), eight notes thereafter were equal in time value to three notes of the same shape before the change occurred.

36. Although "hemiola" is equated with "fifth" by Tinctoris, the former was the common term for a proportion of time, in this case a shift of rhythmic grouping from three notes to two notes of the same value, as in the change from 6/8 to 3/4 meter, in terms of modern notation. In the notation of the period, hemiola was usually indicated by coloration (see note 18), since the change involved was essentially that of making notes imperfect which were normally perfect.

37. *Epogdous* (Gr., "one and an eighth") refers to the intervallic ratio of the interval of the major second. It was used in this sense by Philolaus (5th-4th centuries, B.C.). Tinctoris consistently spells the word *epigdous* (or *epygdous*).

38. The word *epitritus* is an uncommon one in early musical treatises. It is a Latinized form of a Greek word meaning "the third in addition" (i.e., in addition to the unit), thus giving the ratio of 4 to 3, which is the vibration ratio of the interval of the perfect fourth.

39. The word *extractio* is probably used here in the meaning of "borrowing," as in the use of a plainchant or secular melody as a cantus firmus.

40. Mutation was the process of changing from one hexachord to another in order to provide for the solmization of melodies whose range exceeded that of a single hexachord; it also provided for the free use of either b flat or b natural in a voice part. The mutation described in this entry would be used in a conjunct melodic line which descended from e' to f, for example, and which included b flat: the performer would think his part from e' down to c' in the hard hexachord, singing *la–sol–fa*, and then make a quick mental adjustment whereby *fa* was changed to *sol* (but at the same pitch—c'), and then proceed downward in the soft hexachord, singing *(sol)–fa–mi–re–ut* (c'–b flat–a–g–f). Twenty-eight mutations were possible, all of which are listed in eighteen entries of the Dictionary. Some of these can be used only in ascending, others only in descending, while still others may be used in either ascending or descending. Tinctoris' *Expositio manus* contains a complex diagram of the mutations (Coussemaker IV, p. 14; Bellermann has a detailed account of their actual use [*JfMW*, 1863, pp. 86-88]. *See Bibliography, page 99*.)

41. In the first of these mutations, the pitch c, which is sung as *fa*

in the hexachord beginning on g, becomes *ut* in the c hexachord; in the second, the pitch f, which is sung as *fa* in the hexachord beginning on c, is changed to *ut* in the f hexachord. In this note, as in all those concerning the mutations that occur from here on, the nature of the pitch-change involved is indicated but not the actual position of the pitches in the gamut.

42. The definition, one of the most cryptic in the Dictionary, really refers to transpositions of the hexachord to unaccustomed degrees, and so requiring the use of notes not in the Guidonian hand in order to conform to the hexachord interval-pattern. Tinctoris gives a simple illustration in his counterpoint treatise. He shows there (Coussemaker IV, p. 124) that, if a hexachord were to be started on F below Gamma ut (see the diagram on p. 78), there would be no proper note for *fa,* since the hand does not include b flat in that part of the gamut. The flat that would be required there would be, as he says, *extra manum* ("outside the [degrees included in the] hand"), and in that sense would be "fictive." The application of hexachord transposition was much more thoroughgoing than this, however, and involved the use of the accidentals f sharp, c sharp, and e flat when *ut* was considered to begin on d, a, and b flat, respectively. The English theorist, John Hothby (d. 1487), erected hexachords even on F sharp and D flat. (See G. Reese, *Music in the Middle Ages.* New York, 1940, p. 382.) Machabey renders this entry differently by translating *propter* as *en dehors de* ("outside of").

43. "Fugue" was the term used in Renaissance writings for what is now called "canon," i.e., a composition, or section of a composition, in strict imitation in all its voices. In Tinctoris' time, the *fuga* was often written out in only one voice, with indications to show where the successively following voices should enter; these indications were often in the form of a puzzle canon. (See note 12.) The word *nomen* as it appears to be used in this definition is used similarly by Tinctoris in the entry *Solfisatio* (q.v.). The latter part of the definition seems to mean that the imitating voice sometimes begins at the unison.

44. "Imperfection" is another characteristic feature of medieval and Renaissance notation, and in some ways is the opposite of *Alteratio* (q.v.). It means that a note in a perfect mensuration, which would normally be equal in value to three notes of the next smaller note-shape, if followed immediately by one of the latter notes, would thereby be made imperfect, i.e., it would be equal in value to only two such notes. The phrase in the definition, "or of part of that note," is not clear. It may be a reference to the fact that a note could also be made imperfect by a note still smaller than one of the next smaller value, such as a long made imperfect by a following semibreve (called *imperfectio ad partem remotam*). The phrase might also mean that the principle of imperfection applies to smaller as well as larger notes.

45. In Ramos de Pareja's *Musica practica* (Bologna, 1482), the author refers to the two kinds of instruments: one "natural" (i.e., the human voice), the other "artificial" (*monochord, cithara, et cetera*). Similar statements occur in other medieval and Renaissance treatises. The

classification was probably made first by Boethius (*De institutione musica*, 6th century).

46. In a Gregorian chant, the beginning is sung by one or more cantors, or by the priest alone, and is called "Intonation" (also the "Incipit"). In liturgical books, the point to which the Intonation extends is marked by an asterisk; the choir enters immediately afterwards. The melodic formula used at the beginning of a psalm-tone is also called an Intonation. (See the section entitled "Rubrics for the Chant of the Mass," in the Preface to the *Liber usualis*.)

47. The entry merely indicates the manner of performance. The word *jubilus*, also called *neuma* (which Tinctoris spells *Neoma*, q.v.), has a definite meaning, referring to the long melisma on the final syllable of the Alleluia of the Proper of the Mass. A characteristic example is seen in the Alleluia for the Mass for Easter Sunday, *Liber usualis*, 1950 ed., p. 779.

48. In the first of these two mutations, the pitch e, which is sung as *la* in the hexachord on g, becomes *mi* in the c hexachord; in the second, the pitch a, which is sung as *la* in the hexachord on c, becomes *mi* in the f hexachord.

49. In the first of these two mutations, the pitch a, which is sung as *la* in the hexacord on c, becomes *re* in the g hexachord; in the second, the pitch d, which is sung as *la* in the hexachord on f, becomes *re* in the c hexachord.

50. In this mutation, the pitch d, which is *la* in the hexachord on f, becomes *sol* in the hexachord on g.

51. In medieval and Renaissance notation, two or more notes were often combined in one symbol, called a "ligature" (from Lat., *ligare*, "to tie"), and the manner in which the symbol was written determined the time value of each note included in the ligature. In the Brussels manuscript, this entry reads slightly differently: *Ligatura est duarum aut plurium notarum ad invicem continua junctura*, "A ligatura is the direct joining together of two or of several notes to each other."

52. See note 5.

53. See the entry *Regula*, also *Spacium*.

54. An error in the printed edition; the Latin text should read: ". . . Capitulum Undecimum" (". . . Chapter XI").

55. See note 2.

56. See the entry *Armonia*, and note 58.

57. See note 58.

58. Of the three words: *melodia, melos,* and *melum, melum* is distinguished from *melos* only through its Latin ending, while *melodia* is a Greek word itself (μελῳδία). In early treatises, the three terms appear to be used more or less interchangeably. The distinction made by Tinctoris is anything but clear, but it is probable that by *melodia* and *melos* (= *armonia*) he refers to the interval character of a melody (i.e., its mode, its diatonic or chromatic character, etc.), without regard to its rhythm, while *melum* (= *cantus*) is the concept of melody that includes both its intervallic and rhythmical features. See M. Appel, *Terminologie in den mittelalterlichen Musiktraktaten* (Bottrop i. W., 1935), pp. 36-38.

59. "Measure" here is not to be taken in the modern sense, for the music of Tinctoris' time, while in measured rhythm based on fixed time relationships between larger and smaller note values, lacked the metrically recurrent accents of the measures of later music; also, the notation of the earlier music lacked the bar lines that later came to be associated with metrical accentuation.

60. In the first mutation of this entry, the pitch e, which is sung as *mi* in the hexachord on c, becomes *la* in the hexachord on g. In the second, the pitch a, which is sung as *mi* in the hexachord on f, becomes *la* in the hexachord on c.

61. In his discussion of the notes and their values (Coussemaker IV, 41-42), Tinctoris says that there are only five notes regularly used in music: the maxim, long, breve, semibreve, and minim. The latter is naturally indivisible, since it is the smallest of the notes. However, under dupla proportion, a note shape of smaller value—the semiminim—may occur, but only in imperfect prolation, so that the minim, unlike the other four notes, is subject only to duple, not triple, division. The semiminim could be formed in two ways: by attaching a small oblique stroke to the end of the stem of a minim, or by blackening the head of the minim. The latter form may be used even when there is no dupla proportion, and also in perfect prolation, in which case the blackened note is not a semiminim but a minim in hemiola rhythm. Tinctoris says that the unskilled mistakenly call the latter a semiminim when it is used in this context.

62. In this mutation, the pitch a, which is sung as *mi* in the hexachord on f, becomes *re* in the hexachord on g.

63. The word "Mass" was formerly used in a more general sense than it is now, and for a long time was the term used for any liturgical office. (See the entry *Officium,* and note 74). It will be noted that in naming the Gloria and Credo, Tinctoris uses as incipits the words which follow the Intonation. (See note 46.)

64. The most commonly used note divisions (mode, time, and prolation) are described in note 11. The word "mode" was also used to designate the division of the largest note value used—the maxim—into longs, a division which was called the "major" mode, as compared with the "minor" mode, the latter being the next smaller division, i.e., of longs

into breves. The word "mode" standing by itself invariably meant the minor mode. The term *maximodus* was occasionally used to designate the *modus major*. The major mode was more theoretical than practical, as the maxim did not occur often enough in the sources of the period to establish the maximode as another rhythmical level, along with (minor) mode, time, and prolation.

65. The word *maior* is obviously lacking here; it occurs in both the Brussels and the Bologna manuscripts.

66. See note 34. This genus of proportion is not stated clearly; what is meant is simply that the smaller of the two numbers always remains one, and the larger is a multiple of it.

67. The term "aliquot" is explained in note 26.

68. The term "aliquant" is explained in note 35.

69. This description and classification of music appears to have originated with St. Isidor of Seville in the seventh century (see Gerbert, *Scriptores ecclesiastici de musica* [1784; facs. ed., Berlin, 1905], I, p. 21). It is found in several treatises between then and the time of Tinctoris.

70. This verse, which was quoted by several medieval and Renaissance theorists, is the beginning of a long didactic poem about music which has been attributed to Guido d'Arezzo. It is printed in its entirety in Gerbert, *Scriptores . . .* II, pp. 25-34. The Brussels manuscript of the Dictionary has a phrase that does not occur in the printed edition: *non operis servitio*, "not as a workservant," which comes just after the word *speculationis*. (See Coussemaker IV, p. 186.)

71. See note 40.

72. *Neuma* was a name used to indicate a melodic formula which served as a mnemonic aid in singing the psalm-tones and their various endings. The *neumae* had characteristic phrases of text in which the first word designated the number of the mode (e.g., *Primum quaerite regnum Dei*, "First seek the kingdom of God") and vocalized endings, as Tinctoris indicates.

73. See the entries, *Cantus simplex planus* and *Cantus simplex figuratus*. The symbols used to represent notes of "indefinite value," such as those of plainchant, differ in appearance from those of mensural music.

74. Tinctoris is merely making a particular observation here. It was customary in Spanish manuscripts to use the word *Officium* rather than *Missa* at the beginning of a Mass. According to Dom Hourlier of Solesmes Abbey, this use of *Officium* was not confined to the Spanish peninsula. See the entry *Missa*.

75. "Perfection," like "alteration" and "imperfection," is a char-

acteristic feature of medieval and Renaissance notation. Perfection means a mensuration in which certain note symbols were divided into three notes of the next smaller value, unless by context they were made imperfect, i.e., reduced to two such values. (See note 44.) Each degree of value—such as long, breve, or semibreve—could be either perfect or imperfect throughout a given piece, regardless of the mensuration of the other degrees. (Modern 6/8 meter is one in which perfect and imperfect mensurations are combined at different degrees of value, i.e., it is duple in its larger degree, and triple in its smaller degree. In Renaissance terminology, it is in imperfect time and perfect prolation.) Also, a single note which was normally imperfect in its mensuration could be made perfect by the addition of the *punctus perfectionis* (see note 3). In Tinctoris' time the mensurations for each note value were usually indicated by meter signs, such as the circle and semicircle, which stood for perfect and imperfect division, respectively, of the breve (see the entries *Circulus perfectus* and *Circulus imperfectus*). The presence or absence of a dot within the circle or semicircle indicated perfect and imperfect prolation (see the entry *Punctus*). Concerning the second meaning of *perfectio* (two entries later), the Brussels manuscript reads thus: *Perfectio est totius cantus aut particularum ipsius conclusio,* "Perfection is the completion of a whole piece, or of any of its sections." (See Coussemaker IV, p. 186.) The word "perfectio" here may also carry with it the concept of ending on a perfect consonance.

76. See note 11.

77. "Major" and "minor," as used in this and the next entry, are the equivalents of "perfect" and "imperfect." It was a convention to use the former terms for prolation and maximode (see notes 11 and 64), and the latter pair for mode and time.

78. The *Proportionale musices* is one of Tinctoris' twelve famous theoretical treatises. It is described in Reese, *Music in the Renaissance* (New York, 1954) (as are the other works of Tinctoris, pp. 140-149); and is printed in Coussemaker IV, pp. 153-177.

79. See note 24 for an explanation of Tinctoris' use of the word *proprietas*. It was employed with quite another meaning by other theorists, viz., in reference to the rhythmical interpretation of ligatures, but never by Tinctoris in this manner in his discussion of ligatures (Coussemaker IV, pp. 42-45).

80. See notes 8, 32, and 75 for explanations of the terms used in the first two sentences of the translation of this entry. The last sentence refers to the dot used in the common sign for a fermata, which has the same appearance today that it had in Tinctoris' time. The use of the term "organ point" for the fermata is noteworthy; in modern terminology "organ point" is the equivalent of "pedal point."

81. Such complex proportions as this and the one in the following entry do not occur in the practical sources of Renaissance music; they do

appear, however, in musical examples especially written to illustrate them, in treatises. (Note, e.g., the entry *Proportio inequalitatis,* in the Dictionary.)

82. This statement occurs in Tinctoris' *Tractatus de regulari valore notarum* (Coussemaker IV, p. 47), and is followed by the explanation that there are four "quantities," i.e., mensurations, namely those of major mode, minor mode, time, and prolation. These are then followed by musical examples which illustrate how each of these quantities is indicated at the beginning of a composition, where they function much as a modern time signature. The symbols used are as follows (in each case perfect and imperfect mensuration, respectively, are given in each mensuration): 1. major mode by either three or two closely set vertical lines, each covering three spaces; 2. minor mode by one vertical line covering either three or two spaces; 3. time by either a full or an incomplete circle; 4. prolation by either the presence or absence of a dot within the circle representing time.

83. Reduction is simply the result of imperfection, in which a larger note in a perfect mensuration is reduced from its normal value of three to two values of the next smaller unit. (See note 44.) In the definition, the term "or their equivalents" (*aut cum sociis*) means that the smaller note which causes the imperfection might be either a single note or a group of notes of still smaller notes equivalent in value to it, the effect in either case being the same.

84. In the first of these two mutations, the pitch a, which is sung as *re* in the hexachord on g, is changed to *la* of the c hexachord; in the second, the pitch d is first sung as *re* in the c hexachord, and then becomes *la* in the hexachord on f.

85. In this mutation, the pitch a, sung as *re* in the hexachord on g, is changed to *mi* in the hexachord on f.

86. See the entry *Cantus compositus,* and note 14.

87. In the first of these two mutations, the pitch d, sung as *re* in the hexachord on c, becomes *sol* in the hexachord on g; in the second, the pitch g, sung as *re* in the hexachord on f, becomes *sol* in the c hexachord.

88. The definition seems to imply that if a composition is to be repeated, the repetition may be as a whole, or only in part, as indicated by a sign in the music.

89. In this mutation, the pitch g, which is sung as *re* in the f hexachord, becomes *ut* in the hexachord on g.

90. See the entry *Diesis,* and note 29.

91. See the entry *Apothome,* and note 5. The apothome is also called the "chromatic semitone," as it occurs between b flat and b natural.

91

92. See the entry *Limma,* and note 29. The limma is also called the "diatonic semitone," as it occurs between e and f (also between b and c), as opposed to the "chromatic semitone" between b and b flat. In this and the previous entry, it appears as though Tinctoris were discussing the three different semitones of the three Greek genera of tetrachords: diatonic, chromatic, and enharmonic. It is more likely, however, that the semitone referred to in the third sentence of the translation is the chromatic raising of f to f sharp, as in the melodic progression g–f–g (even though no sharp was notated), which was a feature of the practice of *musica ficta.* Bellermann was puzzled by this entry (JfMW, 1863, p. 102-103), particularly by the word *sustinetur* (*sustinere* = to "hold up," "restrain," "delay"), but Machabey (*Lexique,* Introduction, ii) has shown that the word was used in several medieval treatises with the meaning "to raise," and in some cases clearly "to raise by a semitone." The sentence where it occurs, then, might be paraphrased as follows: "Under certain circumstances, the chromatic semitone is employed in a voice part to change a melodic interval from a whole- to a half-step, in order to produce a smoother melodic flow."

93. See note 16.

94. This entry and the two that follow make use of the prefix *sesqui-,* Lat. "a half in addition," although the meaning of the prefix is not literally applied except in *sesquialtera.* In all cases it refers to proportions in which the greater number is larger by one than the lesser number, and which are classed together as *superparticulare* proportions. *Sesquialtera,* represented by the figure 3 over 2, is a rhythmical change that occurs very often in Renaissance music. Its effect, when introduced into an imperfect mensuration, is the same as that of a triplet indication in modern notation, i.e., after that point, three notes are equal in value to two notes of the same shape before that point. *Sesquialtera* and *hemiola* are the usual terms for this ratio when applied to time value, *diapenthe* for the interval ratio. (See note 34.)

95. *Sesquitertia* is a proportion represented by the figure 4 over 3; *epitritus* is the Greek term sometimes used by theorists for this proportion (Tinctoris has an entry for this word), while *diatessaron* is this same ratio applied to pitch intervals. Examples of *sesquitertian* may be seen in Apel, *The Notation of Polyphonic Music* (Cambridge, 4th ed., 1953)— one from Tinctoris' *Proportionale musices* (p. 153, Facsimile 33D), and another from Gafurius' *Practica musicae* (p. 162).

96. *Sesquiquarta* is represented by the figure 5 over 4. In Tinctoris' *Proportionale musices,* the entire discussion of this proportion is the same as that given in the Dictionary, but is augmented by a musical illustration (Coussemaker IV, p. 162).

97. In the musical theory of Tinctoris' time, syncopation was not regarded as it is today—as a shift of accent from its normal place on a strong beat—but rather as the splitting of a group of notes (equivalent to a modern measure) by the insertion of a single larger note equal in

92

value to that group. Thus in the rhythm of quarter-half-quarter (in duple time), the two quarter notes would have been considered as a unit which had been begun, but which was then interrupted by the interpolation of another unit (the half), and then completed by the second quarter note.

98. In the mutation *sol-fa*, the pitch c, which is *sol* in the hexachord beginning on f, is sung as *fa* in the hexachord on g.

99. In this mutation, the pitch d, which is *sol* in the hexachord on g, is sung as *la* in the hexachord beginning on f.

100. In the first of the two mutations on *sol-re*, the pitch d, which is *sol* in the hexachord on g, is sung as *re* in the hexachord on c; in the second, the pitch g, which is *sol* in the hexachord on c, is sung as *re* in the f hexachord. There is an error in this definition: The word *descendendum* should read *ascendendum* (hence the word "descend" in the translation should read "ascend"). The definition is correct in the Brussels manuscript. (See Coussemaker IV, p. 188.)

101. In the first of the two mutations on *sol-ut*, the pitch g, which is *sol* in the hexachord on c, is sung as *ut* in the hexachord on g; in the second, the pitch c, which is *sol* in the hexachord beginning on f, is sung as *ut* in the c hexachord.

102. This word is spelled *schema* in Coussemaker (IV, p. 189), and is nowadays spelled *schisma*. It refers to the smallest interval considered in acoustical studies (two cents), and it cannot be recognized by the ear. Tinctoris' description of it as an interval does not accord with the usual statements concerning its size. (See the entry "Comma" in Apel, *Harvard Dictionary*. Cambridge, 1954.)

103. The proportions in this and the next entry differ from any other entries in the Dictionary which treat of proportions, all of which represent some degree of diminution. Those with the prefix *sub-*, however, represent the opposite—augmentation—since they increase the values of the note symbols when they are introduced into the music. Thus, under *subdupla* proportion, represented by the figure 2 under 1, a given note symbol would have twice its previous value after this sign occurred.

104. *Submultiplex* is the general species of proportion of which *subdupla*, the previous entry, is an individual kind. In *submultiplex proportion*, the smaller of the two numbers always remains one (1 over 2, 1 over 3, 1 over 4, etc.) while the larger is a multiple of it. Cf. the entry *Multiplex*.

105. In the Brussels manuscript (Coussemaker IV, p. 189), this entry begins: *Superacutae claves, superacuta loca, et superacutae voces . . . .*, thus paralleling the entries *Acutae claves . . .* and *Graves claves. . . .*

106. *Superbipartiens* is a subspecies of proportion included under the general class called *superpartiens* (see note 108). In *superbipartiens,*

the first of the two numbers making up the ratio is always larger by two than the smaller number. The ratio 5 over 3, cited in this entry, is illustrated by a musical example in Tinctoris' *Proportionale musices* (Coussemaker IV, p. 163).

107. *Superparticulare* refers to a kind of proportion that includes all ratios in which the first of the two numbers is larger by one than the smaller number. *Sesquialtera* (q.v.) is the most commonly used proportion of this type.

108. *Superpartiens* is a general type of proportion in which the first of the two numbers making up the ratio is larger by more than one than the smaller number. Tinctoris gives several examples of various subtypes of this proportion in the chapter "De genere superpartiens" of his *Proportionale musices* (Coussemaker IV, pp. 162-165).

109. In the fifteenth century, special systems of notation for instrumental music came into being—the tablatures, which differed considerably from the notation of vocal music in their use of signs to indicate pitch, rhythm, etc. It is likely that this is what Tinctoris refers to as "substitution" for the usual manner of notating music. The word *suppositio* is rare in early treatises.

110. Both Bellermann and Machabey translate *supremum* as "soprano," its equivalent in modern terminology, although the latter word does not appear to have made its appearance in music until the early eighteenth century. *Superius, Cantus,* and *Discantus* are terms more commonly used to designate the highest voice in a polyphonic composition than *Supremum;* the latter word occurs previously in the Dictionary under the entry *Contratenor.*

111. The word "Tetragrammaton" (Gr. "the word of four letters") was used in the late Middle Ages as a mysterious symbol for the name of God. It refers specifically to the Hebrew word "Yhwh" (vocalized as "Jehovah"), but, as Bellerman indicated, the letter "T" also stands for *Theos* (Gr. "God"), which is actually a four-letter word also, as "Th" is represented in Greek by a single letter.

112. Cf. the entry *Color. Talea* refers particularly to a rhythmic pattern which is repeated throughout one voice part of a composition, usually the Tenor. Tinctoris' definition applies primarily to the isorhythmic motet in its final stage, in which both *talea* and *color* coincided in length, but in an earlier period composers often caused them to overlap.

113. See note 11.

114. The emphasis on the Tenor reflects the traditional importance of this part in carrying the cantus firmus, especially in sacred compositions.

115. See the entry *Arsis,* and note 7.

94

116. See the entry *Diesis,* and note 29.

117. "Consonance" is obviously an error; the word intended is "dissonance," as indicated by Tinctoris under the entry *Tonus equivocum* . . . (q. v.). The Brussels manuscript has the correct word "discordantia" here. (See Coussemaker IV, p. 189.)

118. See the entry *Intonatio.*

119. "Mode" here refers to the varying intervallic character of each of the eight church modes; these are defined in the entries which follow.

120. The entries describing the eight church modes appear to be contradictory in some respects to the accepted tradition of the modes, but a closer inquiry into Tinctoris' definitions reveals that the contradictions are only apparent; they result from an unfortunate combination of ambiguity of statement plus errors of omission. The modes are considered in detail by Tinctoris in his third treatise, *Liber de natura et proprietate tonorum* (Coussemaker IV, p. 16). The formation of each of the modes is indicated there in the usual manner, i.e., it is stated that the four authentic modes (nos. 1, 3, 5, and 7) are those formed by scale segments comprising a fifth—ascending from each of the four notes d, e, f, and g—and in addition a scale segment of a fourth which is added above that. The corresponding plagal modes (nos. 2, 4, 6, and 8) are formed by the same fifths, but with the fourth segment added below. Each mode-pair (1-2, 3-4, 5-6, and 7-8) has the same final, and the normal ambitus of each mode is an octave. The final and its octave, then, define the limits of each authentic mode, while the final lies in the center of the plagal modes.

The entries in the Dictionary, however, seem to say that the authentic modes can descend below the final by the distance of either a major or a minor third, and that the plagals can ascend above the final by the distance of either a major or minor seventh. This is contrary to the usual teachings in respect to both range and use of accidentals, the latter being excluded from the modes, except for the occasional use of b flat. However, Tinctoris' statements concerning the ranges are correct in the light of what he writes in the treatise mentioned above (Coussemaker IV, p. 28), where he refers to a certain "license" that was allowed in extending the regular (octave) ranges of both the authentic and the plagal modes, as described in the Dictionary. Should this extension continue one degree further, however, the mode will have lost its identity as either a plagal or authentic, and is then considered to be a "mixed" mode, combining the ranges of both.

The statement that each authentic can descend either a major or minor third below the final, and that each plagal can ascend a major or minor seventh above the final, implies the use of several accidentals that are foreign to the modes, and can only be explained in the following manner: Tinctoris has for some reason applied to the description of each mode a general rule that applies to the modes as a whole. In the authentic modes, e.g., the third below is said to be either major or minor, but actually there is no choice for any given mode—the third below is minor in modes 1, 5, and 7, and major in mode 3. In the plagal modes, the seventh above is minor in modes 2, 4, and 8, but major in mode 6.

The difficulties in comprehending Tinctoris' meanings have been compounded by the fact that in the entries concerning modes 1 and 2 certain words are obviously lacking. A comparison of the eight entries shows that the description of mode 1 lacks the two words *vel semiditonum* ("or minor third"), which appear in all the other entries concerning the authentic modes; the description of mode 2 lacks the phrase *ac diatessaron descendere* ("and descend a fourth"), which appears in all the other entries concerning the plagal modes. The missing words of both entries actually occur in the Bologna and Brussels manuscripts. Certain other omissions have been added in brackets to the translations of the entries describing the first four modes; these additions complete the explanations in a parallel manner to those of the last four, which includes the species of the fourths as well as of the fifths in those modes.

The various "species" of fourths and fifths referred to in the mode descriptions are classifications based on the various positions of the semitone in each scale segment, and are explained by Tinctoris in Chapter II of his mode treatise, *De speciebus diatessaron ac diapenthe,* Coussemaker IV, pp. 19-20. The reason why modes 5 and 6 are said to be formed by either the third or the fourth species of the fifth is that b flat sometimes occurs in these modes, thereby shifting the position of the semitone. With b flat the fifth would be of the fourth species, whereas with b natural it would be of the third species.

121. Irregular endings occur frequently in the eight psalm-tones, most of which are provided with various finals so that the end of each psalm may be smoothly connected to each of the various Antiphons with which it is joined.

122. See note 123.

123. A *tonus commixtus* is a mode which, if authentic, changes during the course of a melody to a mode other than its own plagal, and vice versa. A *tonus mixtus* is a mode which employs the whole range—both authentic and plagal—of any mode pair.

124. In discussing the modes, theorists did not always agree on the use of certain terms. Ramos de Pareja, e.g., in his *Musica practica* (1482), objects to the use of the word *plusquamperfectus.* He prefers to call modes of both more and less than an octave in range "imperfect," the former "by superfluity," the latter "by deficiency."

125. *Tripla* is a proportion of diminution in time. It is represented by the sign of 3 over 1, and, when introduced into the music, means that a given note symbol has one-third the value it had before that point.

126. The *triplum* would be the highest voice in a three-part composition and the next highest in a four-part one. The word arose in the thirteenth century, when the parts above the Tenor (then the lowest voice) were called the *Duplum, Triplum,* and *Quadruplum,* in ascending order. In this connection see the entry, *Supremum.*

127. I.e., tones produced by voices are "natural," those produced by instruments "artificial." See the entry, *Instrumentum,* and note 45.

128. In the first of these two mutations, the pitch c, which is *ut* in the hexachord on c, is sung as *fa* in the hexachord on g; in the second, the pitch f, which is *ut* in the hexachord on f, is sung as *fa* in the hexachord on c.

129. In this mutation, the pitch g, which is *ut* in the hexachord on g, is sung as *re* in the hexachord on f. The word *ascendendum* in the definition should read *descendendum,* and the translation should read "descend" at the corresponding place. This error also occurs in the Brussels manuscript (see Coussemaker IV, p. 191).

130. In the first of these mutations, the pitch g, which is *ut* in the hexachord on g, is sung as *sol* in the c hexachord; in the second, the pitch c, which is *ut* in the c hexachord, is sung as *sol* in the hexachord on f.

131. Two of the five entries in the Brussels manuscript—*Diacisma* and *Scisma*—which are not found in the printed edition are not actually additions, but substitute terms in the latter for the entries *Diastema* and *Stema,* respectively. The definitions of *Scisma* and *Stema* are identical. *Diacisma* is called "half of the lesser semitone," while *Diastema* is defined in the printed edition as "comma." Since "comma" is defined in both manuscript and printed edition as "the difference between two lesser semitones and a whole tone," and since a whole tone is said to be equal to five *dieses* and the lesser semitone to two *dieses,* it follows that both comma and diacisma are considered equivalent to one *diesis.* Concerning the size of the *diesis,* however, see the following entry.

132. The significance of this definition lies in its statement that the actual size of the *diesis* was a matter of disagreement among theorists of Tinctoris' time, which is not indicated in the definition given in the printed edition (q.v.). The name "Thomas" in this entry may refer to St. Thomas of Aquinas (1225-1274) who, according to Eitner (*Quellenlexikon*), wrote a theoretical treatise, *De arte musica,* which exists in a manuscript at the University of Ticinum, Italy, and was published at Milan in 1880. The "philosopher" referred to is Aristotle.

133. See notes 131 and 132.

134. This is the third of the three hexachord definitions (the others being *B durum* and *natura*) which is unaccountably missing from the printed edition of the Dictionary. See note 10.

135. The word "number" is defined in a similar manner in another treatise of this period, *Musica* (1490) by Adam von Fulda, in which Chapter II of the section on proportions begins thus: *Numerus est multitudo ex unitatibus constituta, quo ablato omnia depereunt.* "A number is a sum composed of [individual] units which, if it is removed, causes all [the units] to disappear." See Gerbert, *Scriptores* . . . , III, 368b. "Num-

ber" is used synonymously with "proportion," as the following sentence (in Chapter III of the same section of Adam's treatise) indicates: *Omnia itaque numerus vel proportio in quinque generibus ordinatur.* . . . "Every number or proportion, therefore, is arranged according to five species. . . ." The five species are *multiplex, superparticulare, superpartiens, multiplex superparticulare,* and *multiplex superpartiens,* all of which are entered in Tinctoris' Dictionary.

BIBLIOGRAPHY

Tinctoris, Johannes. *Terminorum musicae diffinitorium*
[Treviso, Gerardus de Lisa, 1495] Hain no. 15527 Quarto, [a-b^8] 16 leaves. Type-page 140 x 93 mm.; 28 lines. a.i recto, title; a.i verso, blank; [a.ii-b.vii] recto, text; [b.vii] verso, colophon; [b.viii] recto and verso, blank. Type 102R

Copies of printed edition recorded at:

Gotha (Landesbibliothek), Munich (Bayerische Staatsbibliothek), Treviso (Biblioteca capitolare), Vienna (Gesellschaft der Musikfreunde), Paris (Bibliothèque nationale—Réserve), London (British Museum), Cambridge (University Library), Washington (Library of Congress)

Copies of the treatise in manuscript recorded at:

Brussels. Bibliothèque Royale (now Bibliothèque Albert Ier) Fétis Collection
No. 5274, fifteenth-century copy of Tinctoris' works
No. 5275, nineteenth-century copy of no. 5274
No. 5276, sixteenth-century copy of *Diffinitorium* and *Proportionale*
Paris. Bibliothèque nationale
Lat. 9338, nineteenth-century copy after Fétis no. 5274
Paris. Conservatoire
B1506 et 7, nineteenth-century copy
B3449, nineteenth-century copy after Fétis no. 5274
Bologna. Conservatorio "G. B. Martini"
B2, fifteenth-century copy

Reprints and translations:

1. Forkel, J. N. *Allgemeine Litteratur der Musik*. Leipzig, 1792, p. 204-16. [In Latin, after the copy at Gotha]
2. Lichtenthal, P. *Dizionario e bibliografia della musica.* Milan, 1826, v. 2, p. 297-313 [Latin after Forkel]
3. Hamilton, J. *Hamilton's Celebrated Dictionary*. London [1849] Appendix. [Latin after Forkel]
4. Bellermann, H., in Chrysander's *Jahrbücher für musikalische Wissenschaft,* I, 1863, p. 55-114 [Latin after Forkel, with German translation and commentary]

5. Coussemaker, E. de (*Scriptorum de musica*. Paris, 1864-76, v. 4, p. 177-81. [Latin after Brussels Ms. Fétis no. 5274]
6. Coussemaker, E. de. *Joannis Tinctoris Tractatus de musica*. Nova ed. Insulis, 1875, p. 416-503 [Latin after Brussels Ms. Fétis no. 5274]
7. Balogh, L. *The Music Dictionary of Johannes Tinctoris*. Unpublished Master's thesis, Western Reserve University, Cleveland, 1940 [English translation after Coussemaker and Bellermann, with notes and bibliographical comments. Includes also a translation of Tinctoris' *Liber de natura et proprietate tonorum*]
8. Machabey, A. *Lexique de la musique* (XVe siècle). Paris [1951] [Latin after Bibliothèque nationale Lat. 9338, with French translation vis-à-vis, notes, introductory comments, and brief bibliography]

THE PRINTING OF TINCTORIS' *DICTIONARY*

Tinctoris' *Diffinitorium* is famous for the wrong reasons. Musicians and bibliophiles, for the last 175 years, have acclaimed it because of its supposed importance in the history of printing, but few have appreciated its substance. Many have termed it the first dictionary of music; others have called it the first printed book on music. It is neither. But the misattributions, the genuine rarity of the book, the author's vocabulary and cryptic style, which have presented many difficulties to those who wish to understand it, have all contributed to a special aura of romance which surrounds the work.

This essay attempts to correct some of those errors about it which have persisted in histories and encyclopedias of music since the eighteenth century. Evidence that would eliminate these errors has been available for some time, but has never been systematically organized and brought specifically to the attention of musicians. It is important to do so, for the fame of the *Diffinitorium* should rest on its content, not on an exaggerated importance given it in the history of printing.

The errors have arisen because the original edition bears no printer's name, place, or date of publication—in short, no imprint. The ink, paper, and format are all unexceptional. So-called internal evidence, upon which some investigators have seized, has led to erroneous conjectures. Today all such methods are as unnecessary as they are fruitless, for reliable typographical evidence is now available which indicates that the *Diffinitorium* was printed in Treviso, Italy, about 1495, by one Gerardus de Lisa, sometimes known as Gerardus de Flandria.

The incunabula he produced are worthy of note, for his

101

presswork was admirable. Almost all music incunabula, however, are interesting and important, for of an estimated 40,000 titles and editions produced by European printers by the end of the fifteenth century, in untold numbers of copies, less than one per cent concern music specifically.

Of this select few, the *Diffinitorium* was for many years the most famous, since it was believed to be the earliest, an eminence for which Dr. Charles Burney is chiefly responsible. In his famous *General History of Music* (Vol. II, p. 458), he mentions finding a copy in the King's Music Library (and taking it to his lodgings for closer study!) to which he assigns a date of about 1475, and which he then dubs "the first printed book on music."

His opinion, and that of others who have stated that the book was printed at about this date, rests on the bethrothal of Princess Beatrice of Aragon, daughter of Ferdinand, the King of Naples and Aragon. To her Tinctoris dedicated the dictionary with the words, "ad illustrissimam Virginem et Dominam D. Beatricem . . . ," a phrase apt before 1475 but inappropriate after Beatrice's marriage to Mathias Corvinus, King of Hungary, in 1476. Burney and others reasoned that Tinctoris would have changed the dedication to honor Beatrice as "Queen of Hungary" had it been written after 1476. That is probably true, but they made the mistake of assuming that printing followed promptly upon the writing of the book.

Burney also decided that the book must have been printed in Naples. He knew that Tinctoris was Ferdinand's chapelmaster from 1476, or earlier, to 1487, and he also knew that Ferdinand and Beatrice had brought a high level of culture, including the art of printing, to the Kingdom as early as 1474, perhaps even before that. It was on this evidence that Burney's erroneous deduction about the place of printing was made. This has not proved as grievous as his error in dating, however, which has been preserved in many standard reference works—Eitner's *Quellenlexikon,* Fétis' *Biographie universelle,* early editions of *Grove's Dictionary,* Barclay-Squire's British Museum *Catalogue,* and in the article about Tinctoris in the *Biographie nationale,* t. xxxv—to name only a few.

Many present-day writers, though not all, have adopted the

102

correct date, 1495. In his recent translation of the dictionary, Armand Machabey still maintains Burney's dating, ". . . imprimé vers 1475," and even implies that a variant printed edition may exist. ". . . l'une des éditions du Lexique. . . ." Only eight years later (1959) Claudio Sartori, in the Ricordi *Dizionario,* amplifies Machabey's conjecture to this: "pubbl. forse a Napoli intorno al 1475, ristampato a Treviso nel 1492." Now we have two editions! But a comparison of three of the eight known copies (those of the Bibliothèque nationale, the British Museum, and the Library of Congress) and detailed descriptions of the others all indicate a complete identity of the extant copies. If one is dated correctly, then all are.

Facts to support the dating of 1495 derive mainly from the work of Victor Scholderer, who has made intensive studies of Gerardus' publications. His long article on Gerardus in *The Library* for 1930 adds details about the printer's life which are germane to a study of any of his works and which also show that he and Tinctoris had much in common. Both were Flemish, Tinctoris being from Nivelles, Gerardus from Ghent, and they were almost exact contemporaries. Gerardus probably moved to Italy before Tinctoris, but by 1476 both had become highly regarded figures there in their respective professions—Gerardus being unchallenged by competitors in the business of printing in Treviso, while Tinctoris, in that year, was elevated to the post of Ferdinand's *capellanus maior.* Gerardus was also a musician, but to him, the true Renaissance man—at various times printer, bookseller, church official, teacher, and debt-collector—distinction in music came only after 1488, when he became choirmaster at the Cathedral in Treviso. Music was never his sole interest or vocation, but his work as choirmaster might have brought him into contact with Tinctoris. Scholderer says that one meeting, perhaps one which renewed an even earlier acquaintance, may have occurred after 1487, when Tinctoris was sent by Ferdinand to recruit choristers in the Low Countries. While Tinctoris did not return to Naples from this journey, he did remain in Italy through the middle of the 1480's, during which time he and Gerardus may have met.

This accords with a date of 1495 for the printing of the

Diffinitorium, obviously, but it is only conjecture. Fortunately, the date can be determined by more tangible, typographical evidence. Most of this is set out in the following chart. While it draws heavily on Scholderer's studies, it also contains additions from other standard works on incunabula.

The bibliographies cited are: VdM = Van der Meersch, *Récherches sur la vie . . . des imprimeurs belges et neerlandais,* 1856; H = Hain, *Repertorium bibliographicum;* C = Copinger's supplement to Hain's *Repertorium;* and GW = *Gesamtkatalog der Wiegendrucke.* 4°, 8°, and F are used not to indicate size, as is customary today, but to note the way signatures in the volume were formed; this is more fully explained later. R and G designations refer to Roman and Gothic styles of type; Gk shows Greek type interspersed with Roman or Gothic. In the imprint column, "f.i." means that the full imprint—date, place, and printer's name—appears somewhere in the book. Bracketed dates are those which have been approximated by reliable means. The names and titles in italics are those important in dating the *Diffinitorium;* since they are mentioned later, they are italicized here only for emphasis. While the chart is not an exhaustive bibliography of Gerardus' productions, it contains all but a few relatively unimportant pamphlets which would in no way affect the dating of the dictionary.

In the numbered categories assigned Gerardus' types, numerals indicate size, letters the style. Size is determined by a standard formula: height of type page in millimeters, times 20, divided by type lines per page. Type styles can be determined visually; few fifteenth-century printers possessed more than one style of Gothic or Roman in any one size. Within each of their limited number of fonts, variants do appear, for type metal in the fifteenth century was soft, and characters wore out rapidly or broke in the press. As a printer cast new type to replenish his cases, minor changes crept into each font. The longer it was in use, the more numerous became the modified faces, and by observing the rate at which those variant type faces appear in a printer's works, we can today deduce with surprising accuracy the order in which they issued from his press. Since at least a few of every printer's productions bear dates, even those lacking dates can usually be fitted into the chronology of his presswork.

Following this procedure, Scholderer states that type 102R, which Gerardus used for the Mahomet volume (undated, but known to have been printed in 1476), is in its earliest state, while in the Pallavicinus, which bears the printed date 1494, it is in its latest, most modified state. Tinctoris' *Diffinitorium* is also set in this latest state of 102R and cannot, therefore, have been printed before, or even near, the date of the Mahomet. In fact, had it been printed about the date 1475 we should expect to find it in 105R, for all the evidence shows Gerardus using this type exclusively at that time.

According to the same evidence, Naples as the place of publication is also erroneous, for type 102R was used only at Treviso, and there in its latest state only after 1492. During his migrant years at Udine, Cividale, and Venice, Gerardus worked with a small Gothic type, 80G, with but one irrelevant exception. The books which are sometimes said to have been printed by him in Naples are, as Scholderer has shown, the work of other printers, as are those from Brescia and Vicenza which are sometimes credited to him.

Other aspects of a printer's work also serve to reinforce judgments made on the basis of type examination, and one of these proves invaluable in helping to pinpoint the date of the *Diffinitorium* within the period during which Gerardus was using the improved and modified 102R. The earliest works produced with movable types were printed one sheet at a time. Volumes consisting of such sheets folded once, in half, are termed "Folio"; those consisting of sheets folded twice are called "Quarto"; those in which the sheets are folded three times, making a smaller volume, are called "Octavo." These various folds form what are called "signatures," and a number of these put together form a book. Keeping them in the proper order during this process is difficult, however, and to avoid errors, printers early began to mark each signature, or certain key ones, with letters or numerals indicating their intended position in the finished book.

Books which have such marked signatures are normally conceded to be later products of the same press than those without, and those with printed signatures later than those marked by hand. This is important in dating the *Diffinitorium,* for though it and the Jacobus correspond in every typographical way to the

PLACE	DATE	PRINTING ACTIVITIES
Treviso	1470	sets up press
	[1470?]	work by: Rolandellus (Vdm No. 3)
	1471	Augustinus
		Phalaris
		Alberti
		Hermes Trismegistus
	[1471?]	Dares (C, ii, 1881)
		"Tormento del beata Simone" (H 15550)
		Tuberinus (H15653)
	1472	Alex. Gallus (C 666)
	1473	Lode de Venezia (C, iii, 4784)
	[1473?]	Varro (C, iii, 5952)
	1474	Latini
		Vincentius Ferrer
		Terentius (H 15406; C, iii, 5745)
		"Vita di Alessandro" M (H 797)
	1475	Alberti
		"Mirabilia Romae"
		Pius II
		Pratus
	[1476?]	*Mahomet*
	1476	Perottus
		"Oratiunculae de communione" (VdM No. 25)
	1477	Guerino, il Meschino
	1478	"Tractatus procuratoris"
Treviso	1478	"Arte del abbaco" (H 1863; GW 2674)
		"Regulae consequentiarum" (C 5095)
Udine	1479	not printing
Cividale	1480	Bartholomaeus de Platina
		Guerinus Veronensis
		Isidorus
Udine	1480	not printing
	1484	"Friuli Statutes"
	1485	Perottus
	[1485?]	Diaconus
		Gratianus
Treviso	1488	not printing
	1492	*Jacobus*
		Haedus
		Crassus (H 5810)
	1494	*Pallavicinus*
	[1495?]	*Jacobus*
		Tinctoris

SIZE	TYPE	OTHER TYPOGRAPHIC FEATURES
—	—	? first work; experimental
8°	105R	f.i.
		f.i.
		place; no printer's name
		f.i.
4°		not in British Museum
—	—	no date; place and printer given
—	—	no date; place and printer given
—	—	place and date; no printer
4°	—	no place or printer given
F	—	no imprint
F	105G	f.i.
4°		printer and date; no place
F	—	date and place; no printer
—	—	date and place; no printer
4°	105GR	f.i.
		f.i.
		f.i.
		f.i.
	102R	undated; colophon "G.F.T."; earliest 102R with single close-set Qu; narrow, straight-shank h; no use of AE.
	102R; Gk	f.i.
—	—	Not in British Museum
F	103R	f.i.
4°	80G	f.i.
—		not in British Museum
4°		not in British Museum
		f.i.
—		not in British Museum
4°		place and date; no printer's name
4°		f.i.
		not in British Museum
8°		cryptic imprint
—		not in British Museum
4°	102R	f.i.; 102R now with single but not close-set Qu, larger h, other changes
4°		f.i.
—	—	f.i.
		place and date; no name. 102R latest state; h appears broken; AE used for first time.
		no imprint; as above, but with printed signatures.

Pallavicinus, which is dated 1494, they carry in addition printed signatures, indicating that they postdate it. They postdate it by only a few months, however, for by 1496 insolvency had overtaken Gerardus, and he moved to Aquileia, where he died in 1499.

No other date except 1495 is reasonable for the *Diffinitorium,* but one perplexing question remains: If the dictionary was printed as late as 1495, why did not Gerardus—perhaps even with Tinctoris' approval, if the two actually did meet—change the dedication to accord with Beatrice's changed status?

Scholderer believes Gerardus' procedures to have been common enough. Printers often printed manuscripts exactly as they came to hand, duplicating not only the text, but sometimes the placement of the text on the page, the decorations and rubrics, and occasionally even the scribal hand itself. They probably did not consider the way history, 100 or 500 years later, might treat them or their productions. The preoccupation with history—both written and yet to be written—with historical accuracy, definitive editions, and authoritative texts, is one of our century. We should refrain from imputing similar concerns to the early printer. In all likelihood Gerardus never imagined that his production of the *Diffinitorium* would survive so long, or cause such confusion. He would doubtless be amazed to learn that we even know of it.

James B. Coover